QUEEN CREEK CANYON

ROADSIDE AREAS

BY CAS SUNDELL

This guide is intended to provide information on finding and identifying routes to date in most of the Road Areas in Queen Creek Canyon. There maybe inaccuracies regarding the routes or protection and you're welcome to contact me with any concerns.

And, as always,

don't be stupid, climbing is as dangerous as you make it.

You assume responsibility for your own safety.

ISBN 979-8-9941046-1-3

QUEEN CREEK CANYON

ROADSIDE AREAS

I-40
Flagstaff
I-17
QUEEN
CREEK
CANYON
I-10
Phoenix
Globe
Superior
US-60
Tucson
I-10

QUEEN CREEK CANYON is a stunning area located four miles east of Superior, Arizona (a quick sixty minute drive from Phoenix). Millions of years of wind and water have carved out perfect pockets and edges in the softer dacite rock creating the perfect climbing playground.

Home to the Phoenix Bouldering Contest, Queen Creek Canyon boasts over 700 sport and trad routes and over 1,200 boulder problems. However, this book is not a comprehensive guide to the area, covering only the routes in the more trafficked crags between milepost 228.5 and 230 in the Road Area. Even in these select areas alone, there's something for everyone -- pockets galore, vertical faces, serious overhangs, cracks, and multi-pitches -- more than enough routes to keep you busy for ages.

GETTING THERE

From Phoenix, take the US-60 east for sixty miles. Once out of the big city the scenic drive will fly by as you wind through the desert landscape. You'll pass the iconic Superstition Mountains, miles of open land studded by saguaros, and eventually the historic Picket Post Mountain. After passing through Superior continue uphill on the highway and then through the tunnel. Upon reaching the light on the other side you'll be officially within Queen Creek Canyon and the beginning of the roadside areas.

ACCESS

Accessing the areas in this book is fairly easy. Everything can be reached with a 2WD vehicle and none of the approaches surpass twenty minutes. All of the roadside areas are located on private property and you're required to register to recreate there legally. Registering does not mean that you endorse the mine or land exchange. It's an extremely simple process that can be done at queencreekclimbing.com. Do it once and you're good to go forever.

Anything within fifty feet of either side of US-60 is a strict 'no climbing' zone and is patrolled by law enforcement. DO NOT establish new routes on the walls alongside the highway. You may notice a few routes that line the highway; these were established decades ago before this rule was in place. There's a few good reasons to avoid climbing these bolted lines with number one being that they're off limits and the police have been known to escort climbers off of them.

While not currently affecting access to any of the crags in the canyon, included in this book or not, the mine looms as a potential threat to the local climbing. For over two decades there has been a struggle over the area between Apache Stronghold and Resolution Copper. In 2014, Congress passed a defense bill containing a rider that mandated the transfer of Oak Flat to the mine. The legal battle only intensified when, after the Forest Service published their final enviornmental impact statement (FEIS) in 2021, the Stronghold filed a lawsuit against the project on the grounds of religious freedom.

Alongside Apache Stronghold's lawsuits, the Access Fund and Arizona Mining Reform have been heading the charge. Arguing that the FEIS is inadequate as it doesn't take into consideration the wide-ranging environmental impacts of the proposed block cave mine. Since then the struggle has been ongoing in court.

If Resolution Copper were able to move forward with their project access to many of the more adventerous climbing areas in the canyon would be lost and many others, if not all, would be seriously affected. More devastating than the loss to the climbing community would be the loss of sacred grounds to the Apache Tribe. While there has never been any contention between the Tribe and climbers and we have always coexisted happily, remember that climbing in the canyon is climbing on holy grounds. To learn more about the fight for Oak Flat, how you can help, and for more recent updates you can find a list of resources on page 72.

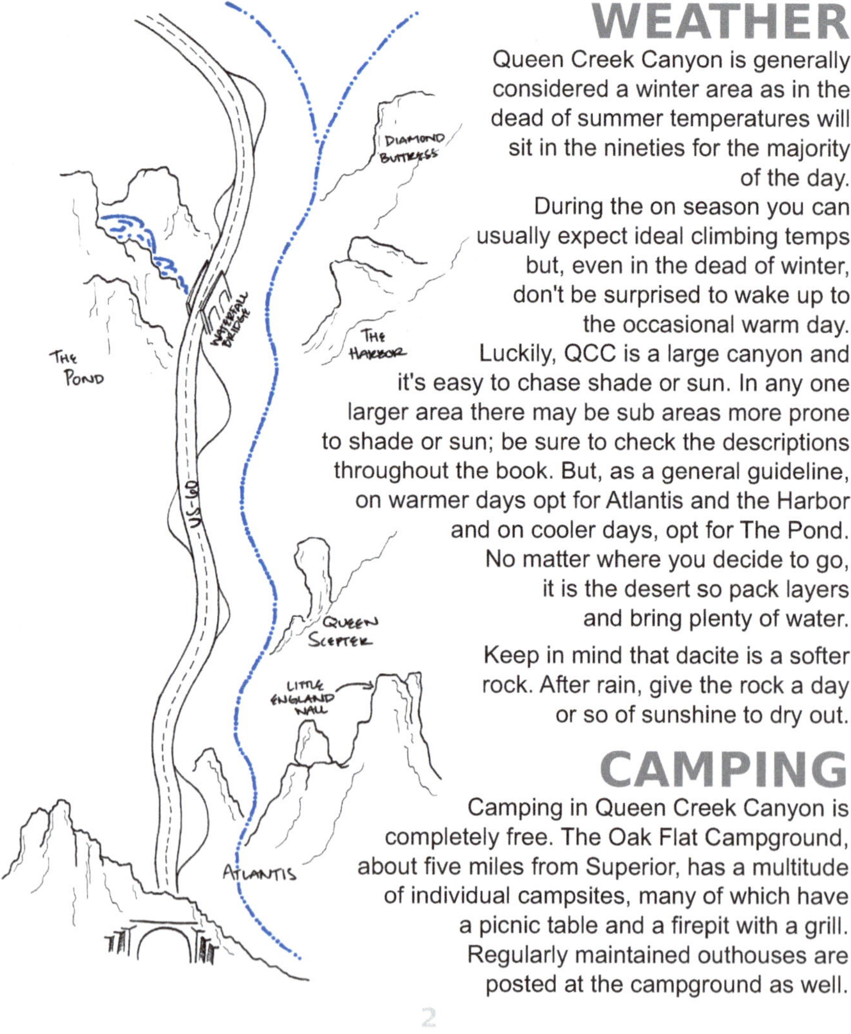

WEATHER

Queen Creek Canyon is generally considered a winter area as in the dead of summer temperatures will sit in the nineties for the majority of the day.

During the on season you can usually expect ideal climbing temps but, even in the dead of winter, don't be surprised to wake up to the occasional warm day.

Luckily, QCC is a large canyon and it's easy to chase shade or sun. In any one larger area there may be sub areas more prone to shade or sun; be sure to check the descriptions throughout the book. But, as a general guideline, on warmer days opt for Atlantis and the Harbor and on cooler days, opt for The Pond.

No matter where you decide to go, it is the desert so pack layers and bring plenty of water.

Keep in mind that dacite is a softer rock. After rain, give the rock a day or so of sunshine to dry out.

CAMPING

Camping in Queen Creek Canyon is completely free. The Oak Flat Campground, about five miles from Superior, has a multitude of individual campsites, many of which have a picnic table and a firepit with a grill. Regularly maintained outhouses are posted at the campground as well.

There is a 14 day stay limit enforced by the USFS.

WATER & FOOD

The nearest water source is down in Superior. For filling up reusable water containers your best bet is the Save Money Market on Main Street. Alternatively, the Dollar General has a water refill station that accepts cards. Circle K also has one that works sometimes.

The Save Money Market is also the best place to go nearby for groceries but if you're looking for more of a selection you'll have to make the 20 mile trip to Globe, where you can find a Fry's and a Walmart.

As for eating out after a long day of climbing, De Marco's, Silver King, Jalapenos, and Porters provide a nice little selection in Superior. Or if you're eastbound, in Globe you'll find La Casita a great place to refuel.

REST DAY ACTIVITIES

HIKING

For days that your fingers are in need of a break but your legs are still good to go there's no lack of hiking in the area.

Closer to Oak Flat there's an abundance of unofficial trails to choose from. There are several dirt roads that depart from the campground which, depending on how far you want to go, can take you on a gentle loop around the campground or all the way to Upper or Lower Devil's Canyon. These roads are occasionally used by vehicles so keep your eyes and ears open. If you're seeking a bit more exploration, you'll find various smaller trails that break away from the dirt roads that lead to the old competition boulders. Even if you're not planning on bouldering it's beautiful and well worth the walk.

In the mood for a bit more of a jaunt and views that are a bit more expansive? You'll find both in the hike to the top of Apache Leap. Park your car at the end of Magma Mine Road at the pull out just before the gate for the mine. Follow the trail down into the wash and onto the dirt road then up and over the hill. At the bottom of the hill look to the right to find a cairned trail leading up the wash. It eventually cuts left, traversing up and over a few washes, before ending at the edge of The Leap. Budget about two hours for the round trip.

On the chance that you're visiting in the spring or fall and you're feeling keen on what could easily be considered the most involved hike -- if it can be called that -- in the area, then the trek out to Five Pools in Hackberry Creek is for you. Though not particularly strenuous in distance or elevation, you'll nonetheless find yourself exerted as you bushwhack and scramble through the downward swerve of layered swimming holes. From US-60 take Magma Mine Road roughly 1.5 miles to a left turn onto FR315. The road is not regularly maintained and a 4WD vehicle is required to drive all the way to the canyon. If lacking access to a capable vehicle, right off the bat you can tack on around three miles of hiking down the road to Lower Devil's Canyon. A quarter mile past the windmill cut into Hackberry Creek and start heading downstream. Just shy of a half mile in you'll encounter a 40 foot dryfall which can be descended fairly easily by zigzagging down ledges. Continue down canyon for a little over half a mile until you reach Lower Devil's Canyon. From there hook a right and continue downstream. There's really no official trail for the next two miles, so choose your own adventure. You'll pass one small waterfall before the canyon veers suddenly east and then immediately west. Shortly after this you'll reach the first pool. If you intend to continue past this pool you'd best be prepared to rappel, downclimb, and/or (depending on the water level) jump, and swim. If you are prepared and willing to do any and all of this, the fourth pool is a real treat.

Budget about eight hours for the round trip.

But wait! There's more! There's no lack of trails in the desert if you're to leave the canyon entirely. Just over ten miles from the campground is Picket Post Mountain with several trails to choose from. Whether you want to head all the way to the top or just circumvent the base you'll find beautiful desert scenery.

Close to Picket Post mountain you can find your way to an old perlite mine after a very short hike; here you may find the odd piece of obsidian as a souvenir. From the campground, drive through Superior and past the Circle K turn left at the sign for the Superior Airport, keep right at every 'V' and eventually you'll find yourself close to the creek and a crude parking lot with some picnic tables. Park here and walk roughly a mile to the old mine.

If you're willing to drive just a little further, the Superstition Mountains have no lack of hiking to offer!

BOYCE THOMPSON ARBORETUM

While still involving a bit of walking, it's much less than any hike. Just eight miles from the campground is Boyce Thompson Arboretum where a $25 admission will let you explore over 1,500 species of desert plants, either on your own or on complimentary guided tours. The Arboretum also offers a range of classes and programs throughout the year so be sure to check their events calendar online to see if anything suits your fancy.

If you find yourself lucky enough to be visiting late March through May, you'll have the opportunity to visit hile most of the plants are blooming!

The Arboretum is open Monday to Thursday 8am-5pm and Friday to Sunday 8am-8pm.

SUPERIOR

For days that both your arms *and* your legs are in need of a break and hiking any length of time sounds unappealing you can surely keep yourself busy the day in downtown Superior. The small downtown is more lively than you might expect. A variety of shops and restaurants worth a visit line Main Street.

Pool tables can be found at Rose's Cantina and the VFW.

The town also has a public pickleball court at the Magma Club at the end of Main Street by the courthouse.

ARIZONA RENAISSANCE FESTIVAL

If you're visiting earlier in the year and you have a penchant for the renaissance then you're in luck! From the first weekend in February to the last weekend in March the Renaissance Festival is open. Located 22 miles west of Superior just off US-60. $36 admission.

GEAR

For the sport routes in the canyon a rack of twenty quickdraws and a 70 meter rope will get you up any line. A few less draws and a 60 meter rope can get the job done on most just be sure to check the bolt count on the route and tie knots in the end of your rope.

An effort is being made to replace the old cold shuts throughout the canyon with updated hardware and mussy hooks. Feel free to contribute time or money for anchor replacements -- see page 72.

For the trad routes in the canyon, recommended gear is listed for each route. Bring more or less as you please. A roadside standard rack (SR) is doubles .3-3 and sm-med nuts.

GETTING THERE

Park at the same pulloff as for Atlantis.

From Superior, head east on the US-60 for 2.5 miles. The parking for The Old Highway is at the pulloff just past the tunnel.

From Globe, head west on the US-60 for 21 miles. The parking for The Old Highway is at the pulloff just before the tunnel.
(33.30597, 111.07797)

At the very west end of the lot you'll see the old highway. Follow the broken asphalt for a few hundred feet. To get to the furthest left routes continue down the road and through the old tunnel.

THE OLD HIGHWAY

The routes in this area are exactly where you'd assume -- along the old highway. The location makes the approach one of the easiest in the canyon. The short cliffband with its notably big ledges and incut edges was a byproduct of the blasting that created the now decomissioned road. Many of the routes are newer and have not been cleaned very well -- beware of choss -- but there are a few standout routes that make it worth the short walk.

You probably won't be able to help but to notice sporadic hardware inside the tunnel as you're passing through. These routes are off limits; please do not climb them! The mine has asked climbers to stay off the rock that is *inside* the old tunnel. We are obliged to do so as they are the ones that own a lot of the land that we climb on elsewhere in the canyon. We would hate to lose access to those areas because people were caught climbing on the very few routes they've asked us to avoid. And if that's not enough incentive for ya, all the routes in the tunnel are on the softest, chossiest rock you'll ever touch in your life -- to be blunt, they suck.

WEST SIDE OF THE OLD TUNNEL

☀ MORNING SHADE

1. Sunset Girl 5.12a ★★

A friable, vertial face. Steep, powerful, committing moves leads to steep crimps. 5 bolts.

FA: Scott Duemler

2. Womb With A View 5.11d PG-13

A mixed line up the broken open book to the face to the right. Three bolts on friable rock lead to an easier section that can be protected with gear. From there head up toward the crux, which you'll find near the end. Take care not to fall off the crux as you'll likely get smashed on the corner below you. Recommended to rap this route to avoid your rope getting sucked into the crack next to the anchors. 7 bolts, .3-1.

FA: Scott Duemler, Aaron Collins

3. Humpty's Route 5.10b PG-13

A mixed line up a dihedral to a smooth face. Start just to the right of the rubble pile on easier terrain and head up to a ledge. From the ledge move onto the thin face then transition left into a crack. 8 bolts, 2-3.

FA: Scott Duemler

4. Bert 5.9 ★

A short, west-facing route to the left of a small gulley. A bouldery start with sustained climbing to the anchors. 6 bolts.

FA: Soren Stauersbol

5. Ernie 5.8 ★

Right line of the two west-facing routes ot the left of the small gulley. Small ledges and small pockets. 6 bolts.

FA: Soren Stauersbol

6. Unnamed Route 5.10 ★

Start to the right of the right-leaning dihedral. A short route on positive crimps. 4 bolts.

FA: Unknown

7. Unnamed Route 5.11b

Bouldery moves on a broken face to a wide arete. 8 bolts.

FA: Mark Harris

8. Unnamed Route 5.10a/b

A bouldery start with a high first bolt (high enough that you shouldn't bother to bust out the stick clip) leads to a sustained face. 9 bolts.

FA: Unknown

9. Craig's Come Over 5.10b/c ★

A bouldery start leads to a run out face. 12 bolts.

FA: Jim A., Leo Bunuel

10. Road Work 5.10d

A mixed line up a broken face to a bulge up high. It is possible, and probably recommended, to bail left below the bulge and finish on the route to the left to avoid passing the halfway mark on your rope. 12 bolts, .3-.75, (130').

FA: Jim A, Leo Bunuel

11. Open Project.

Crack to a ledge with one bolt.

12. RC Chimney 5.4 ★

In the chimney to the left of Dry Bones. Furthest bolted line in the back of the chimney. 6 bolts.

FA: Rachel Drummonds

13. AC Chimney 5.7 ★

In the chimney to the left of Dry Bones. Right route of the two bolted lines in the back of the chimney.

FA: Soren Stauersbol

14. Dry Bones 5.6

Leftmost route on the wall to the left of the west end of the tunnel. Bouldery moves on a short, crispy face. 5 bolts.

FA: Monika Koehler

15. Elevator to the Sun Deck 5.5

Short but extremely run out face. 1 bolt.

FA: Jim A, Leo Bunuel

16. Peach's Face 5.8 ★

Second pitch of Elevator to the Sun Deck. Follow pockets and thin edges up a crispy face.

FA: Taylor Drummonds

17. Princess Crack 5.6 (T) ★★

Second pitch variation of Elevator to the Sun Deck. Obvious crack departing from the anchors of the 5.5. .75-4.

FA: Taylor Drummonds

18. I Don't Care

Short, chossy face. 3 bolts.

FA: Jim A, Leo Bunuel

19. Unnamed Route 5.7 R

Rightmost route to the left of the west end of the tunnel. Every move is 5.7 but all of them are on portable holds. 7 bolts.

FA: Jim A, Leo Bunuel

20. Tunnel Vision 5.10a ★★

About 50' to the right of the west end of the tunnel; some scrambling is required to get to the base of the line.
Follow the right leaning bolt line to a cruxy open book. From there head up past the top of the seam to the anchors.

FA: John Zanini, Ben Ramsey, Dave Gunn

EAST SIDE OF THE OLD TUNNEL

☀ EVENING SHADE

21. AZ Cheetah 5.11d ★★

Furthest left route on the east side of the tunnel. A powerful start leads to thin face climbing.

FA: Soren Stauersbol

22. Hang 10 5.11c ★★

A short but stout route. Start on the sharp arete and head up through the low crux to a no-hands rest before finishing on easier climbing. 4 bolts.

FA: Scott Duemler

23. RZR 5.7

Climbs the easier, ledgy face to the right of the sharp arete. Stem up on jugs but be aware of the abundance of portable holds on this route. 4 bolts.

FA: Soren Stauersbol

24. Rack of Ribs 5.10b ★★

Leftmost route on the first outcropping of rock you'll come to from the parking lot. Climbs the broken face. 7 bolts.

FA: Scott Duemler

25. Horny 5.10a ★

Starts in a short dihedral and then trends left onto the broken face. 5 bolts.

FA: Scott Duemler

26. Stone's Throw 5.9 ★

Big pockets and edges up a vertical face to a cruxy bulge. 5 bolts.

FA: Scott Duemler

GETTING THERE

From Superior, head east on the US-60 for 2.5 miles. The parking for Atlantis is at the pulloff just past the tunnel.

From Globe, head west on the US-60 for 21 miles. The parking for Atlantis is at the pulloff just before the tunnel.

(33.30597, 111.07797)

The trail starts at the west end of the lot. A well-worn path leads down into the canyon.

ATLANTIS

While there's no lack of walls that get their fair share of sun, Atlantis is best known for its shady corridor with routes that stay cool all day long, making the steep lines with big bulges and roofs ideal for pulling hard.

Although the first crack ascents were made in the main area in the early 1970s by climbers on their way to the Little England Wall, it wasn't for another 20 years that someone hauled a drill down and started putting in the first bolts. Since then the area has become a sport climbing playground. You'll find no shortage of well-bolted routes at any grade.

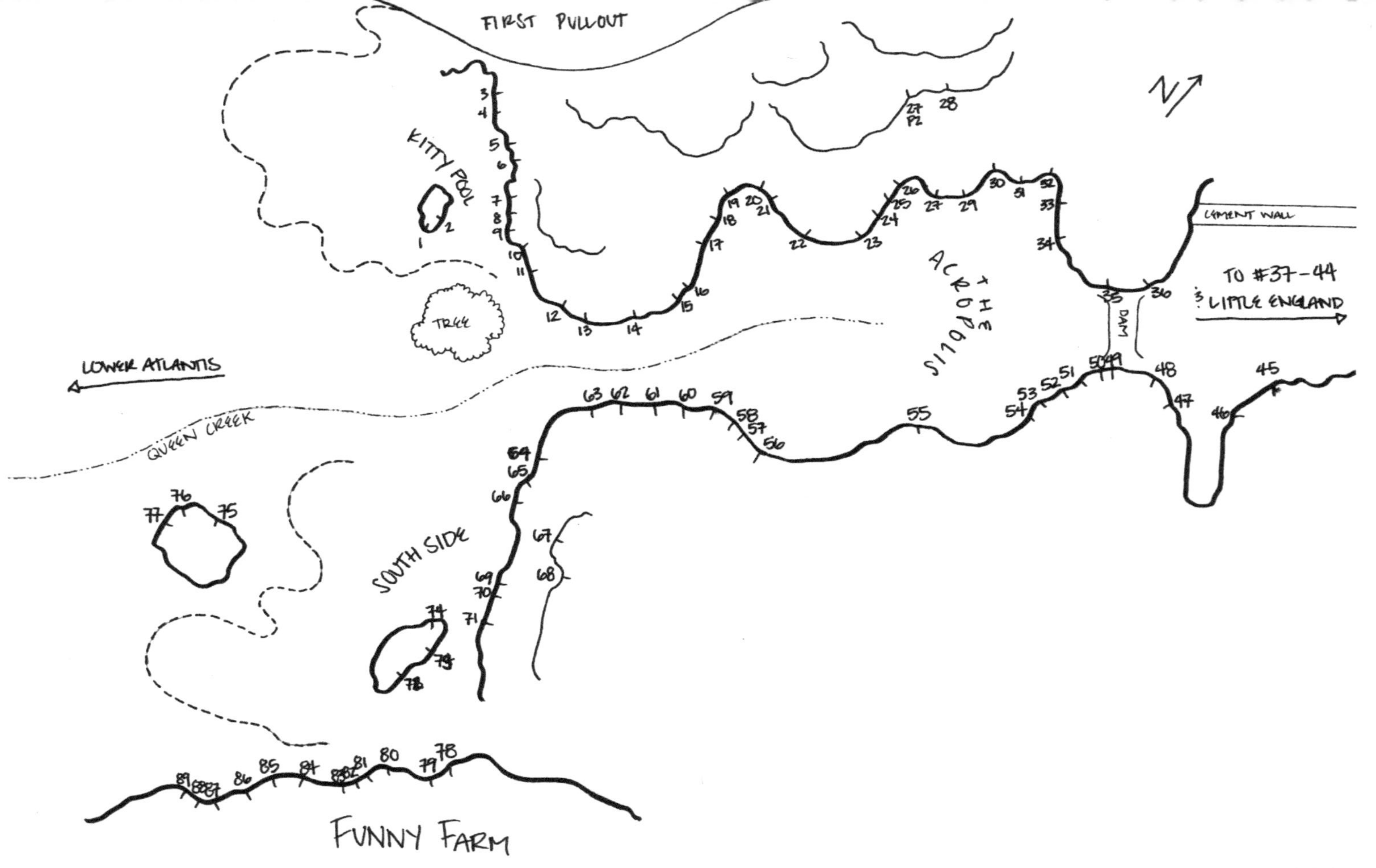

FIRST PULLOUT
KITTY POOL
TREE
LOWER ATLANTIS
QUEEN CREEK
THE ACROPOLIS
DAM
CEMENT WALL
TO #37-44 & LITTLE ENGLAND
SOUTH SIDE
FUNNY FARM

THE KITTY POOL

☀ MORNING SHADE

The routes at The Kitty Pool are the first you'll run into on the trail. Before you reach the riverbed and sycamore tree there will be a short wall to your left (home to routes 1-2) and, once at the end of the trail, the wall facing you comprises the rest of the area.

The Kitty Pool gets morning shade followed by sun for the rest of the day. Even in the middle of winter you can usually count on warm rock in the afternoon.

1. Chicken Star Rocket 5.8+ ★

An easy arete leads to a ledge. Crux is through the bulge, then continue up the face to the anchors. 3 bolts.

FA: Scott Duemler, Michael Genovese

2. Alright Aret-e 5.8 ★

Just around the corner from Chicken Star Rocket. Make your way up over a series of bulges. 4 bolts.

FA: Scott Duemler, Michael Genovese

3. Pollywog 5.6

On the main Kitty Pool wall at the very top of the chossy gulley. 4 bolts.

FA: Scott Duemler, Michael Genovese

4. Highdive 5.9 ★

Toward the top of the gulley. Look for a ledge with some catclaw on the left side. Technical climbing through a short dihedral then pull through the bulge on jugs. Ends with a classic funout to the top (easy 5.5 but run out climbing leads to the anchors). 4 bolts.

FA: Scott Duemler, Michael Genovese

5. Water Wings 5.8 ★

Shares the first five bolts with Monkey Wrench Gang (fourth line from the right). Optional runner on the fifth bolt if you have it, then head up and left toward the vertical headwall. Keep toward the arete to the anchors. 13 bolts.

FA: Scott Duemler, Michael Genovese

6. Monkey Wrench Gang 5.7+ ★★

Fourth line from the right, starts just around a left-facing corner. Fun, vertical climbing through a good variety of holds. 6 bolts.

FA: Jared Putterman, Scott Duemler, Michael Genovese

7. Gonzo Bacon 5.7 ★

Left of the two routes on the clean face next to the sycamore. Vertcial face climbing to a short crack. 5 bolts.

FA: Scott Duemler, Michael Genovese

8. Or, Another 5.7 ★

Right of the two routes on the clean face next to the sycamore. Follow pockets and good edges to the anchors. Shares the last bolt and anchors with Gonzo Bacon. 5 bolts.

FA: Scott Duemler, Michael Genovese

9. Ride the Wave 5.8 ★★

Start up the first four bolts of Or, Another. Recommended to use a runner on the fourth bolt before cutting out right toward the arete and continuing up toward the roof at the top. At the roof, pull around right through some exciting, exposed moves to the anchors. 9 bolts.

FA: Scott Duemler, Michael Genovese

10. For Some Reason 5.7 (T) ★★

The first crack system you encounter at the bottom of the trail. Make your way up the dihedral by stemming, jamming the handcrack, and utilizing the occasional good hold on the face up to the tricky bulge and the anchors. *SR, 4.*

FA: Unknown

11. Water Wait 5.10b ★

The short face just to the right of the crack, easily distinguished by the huge eye bolt in the middle of the face. Choose your own adventure to the first bolt then make your way up the slightly overhung face on crimps and pockets to the final pull over the little roof. 3 bolts.

FA: Scott Duemler, Michael Genovese

NORTH SIDE OF THE ACROPOLIS

☀ MORNING & EVENING SHADE

The Acropolis is home to some of the best rock and best climbs Atlantis has to offer. From the bottom of the trail, make your way into the river bed and head east for just a few steps. That is, if you can! Following heavy rain it can be difficult and sometimes impossible to access the routes in the bowl. The water swallows up any space you'd want to belay and sometimes even the first bolts of the routes. However, when it's dry you can expect easy shade-chasing, great temps, and great routes.

12. Stolen Valor 5.11b ★★★

The obvious overhang at the bottom of the trail. Clip the first bolt from the ground, then move right and make your way up the ramp to the overhang. The second bolt can be reached from a nice, incut undercling then make a couple long moves to a jug for the third. Continue up to a tricky second overhang and from there it's smooth sailing to the anchors. Shares the last four bolts and anchors with Double Cross. 11 bolts.

FA: Cas Sundell, Charlie Brown

13. Double Cross 5.10a ★

Just to the right of the overhang. Start on crimps and make your way up through a tricky bulge and short crack. Once you pull onto the face expect easier climbing to the anchors. Shares the last four bolts and anchors with Stolen Valor. 9 bolts.

FA: Scott Duemler, Michael Genovese, Shawna Greiner

14. Brush Your Teeth Before You Kiss Me 5.9 ★★★

Start under a small roof and follow the crack, utilizing the juggy sidepulls, until you can traverse right onto the face. A nice combination of slab and vertical face climbing leads to an exciting, albeit heady, bulge. Fun moves on big holds will get you to the ledge past the bulge; from there, just a few more moves to the anchors. 10 bolts.

FA: Jay Clark, Mark Harris

15. Crack of Don 5.10b (T) ★★

Start up the slippery slab to the vertical hand crack. Follow the crack as it widens into a flaky off-width, then to a roof that is easier than it appears. Two bolt anchor. *SR, 4, optional 5.*

FA: Don O'Kelley, Kent Brock

16. Public Hanging 5.11c ★★★★

Start over a small roof on the river-polished rock and follow the slab to the vertical face above. Traverse out right under the second roof and pull the crux into the open book feature. The third roof is easier than it might appear and from there, cruise to the anchors. (Note: Originally was done as a mixed route: skip the first small roof and initial three bolts and climb the crack feature slightly to the left of the sport start. Traverse over right at bolt four and continue up.) 11 bolts.

FA: Jim Steagall

17. Capital Punishment 5.12b ★★★

Shares the first three bolts with Armed and Dangerous. Pull through tricky moves in the dihedral to the right of the bolt line then head up the face. Cut left at the third bolt. After the good ledge the route steepens. Compression moves, a nice pocket, and a fixed draw get you through the crux and to a small roof. 9 bolts.

FA: Jim Steagall

18. Armed And Dangerous 5.11b ★★★

Bolt line just to the left of the corner. Shares the first three bolts with Capital Punishment. Pull through tricky moves in the slick dihedral to the right of the boltline then head up the face. From the good rest ledge head up the steep face on pockets and sloping edges until you reach the right-leaning crack. Continue up, using the crack and incut pockets to the left of it. 11 bolts.

FA: Jim Steagall, Eric Hanson

19. Unnamed Crack 5.7 (T) ★

Scramble up the ramp, traversing left toward the corner. Climb the blocky, wide crack just to the right of Armed and Dangerous. Use the anchors for Armed and Dangerous but be sure to bring runners to extend your anchor. *Doubles through 4.*

FA: Unknown

20. Kent's Crack 5.9 (T) ★

Make your way up the ramp (option to start the same as Capital Punishment and Armed and Dangerous but doing so is harder than 5.9), traversing left across the slick rock to the crack in the corner. Climb the right of the two cracks (the crack just to the left of Feast and Famine). Traverse left at the top to the anchors for Feast and Famine. *Doubles through 4.*

FA: Kent Brock, Don O'Kelley

21. Feast and Famine 5.11a ★★★

First bolt line to the right of the corner. Climb up the ramp, traversing left to the first bolt. Enjoy the two distinct roof cruxes separated by easier climbing in the middle. 9 bolts.

FA: Ken Mills, Jim Steagall, Eric Hanson

22. Phantom 5.12a ★★★

Start up the slab on the right side of the obvious bulge. Shares the first bolt with Fluid Dynamics. The crux is pulling through the bulge, then climb through sidepulls, crimps and big moves to gain the lower angle rock above. The rest of the route is airy and may look intimidating but there's good holds all the way. 9 bolts.

FA: Jim Steagall, Eric Hanson, Dave Sobocan

23. Fluid Dynamics 5.12c ★★★★

Shares the first bolt with Phantom. Start up the slab and pull through the low crux on the right side of the bulge and onto the slab above. Traverse right, below the white scooped overhang, then continue up the arete and overhang. A second crux comes at the top of the overhang then follow the vertical, pocketed face to the anchors. 10 bolts.

FA: Jim Steagall, Dave Sobocan, Eric Hanson

24. All the King's Men 5.12d ★★★

Climb up the low angle face below the roof to a high first bolt. Climb out the roof and pull over the lip to an overhanging, bulgy section then (finally) onto a vertical face. 10 bolts.

FA: Jim Steagall

25. Deliver Us 5.13c/d ★★

Alternate start to All the King's Men. Start up the crack in the corner to the right of All the King's Men (same start as Trinity Is My Name) until you reach a bolt out left. Clip the bolt and climb left, squeezing the compression roof block. Finish on All the King's Men. *.1-.75, draws.*

FA: Richie Winter

26. Trinity Is My Name 5.10b/c (T) ★★★

Climbs the thin crack in the corner to the right of All the King's Men. Start up the thin crack and follow it over several roofs as it widens to good hands. Option to traverse to the right at the top and lower off the Neptune anchors or continue up a second pitch to the top of the canyon; in this case rap down the two pitches of Neptune to descend. Note that you need someone to follow Trinity Is My Name to retrieve gear. *SR.*

FA: Manny Rangel, Chris Raypole

27. Neptune 5.10a ★★★★

An exciting start on the slick rock leads to a fun broken face. High clip the fixed

draw at the seventh bolt from incut crimps and then head into the right facing dihedral. 9 bolts.
Less trafficked is a short, three bolt second pitch that leads to the very top of the canyon, traversing up and left from the anchors.

FA: Ken Mills, Dave Sobocan

28. Neptune Direct 5.10a ★★★★

A direct finish to Neptune. From the anchors continue straight up where the original second pitch bailed left into the corner. Fun friction slab to the top of the canyon.
This variation to the finish allows both pitches to be climbed as one but it is a full 35 meters. Even with a 70 meter rope be careful lowering. 5 bolts.

FA: Charlie Brown

29. Impending Doom 5.10d ★

Start around the corner from Neptune up the slick face to a ledge. From there climb up the clean face to the anchors. Avoid the wall to the right -- if you stem back, knock a couple letter grades off. 10 bolts.

FA: Jim Steagall, Eric Hanson

30. Unknown Crack 5.8 (T) ★

Climbs the dihedral just to the right of Impending Doom. Start up the slick face, option to clip the first few bolts for Impending Doom, and from the ledge start up the crack. At the top, step left to use the anchors for the sport route. *SR.*

FA: Don O'Kelley, Kent Brock

31. Schizophrenic Boulevard 5.10c 

The vertical face just left of the big roof. Climb up the river-polished face to the first bolt after the ledge. Crimpy, vertical face climbing for 7 bolts.

FA: Eric Hanson, Jim Steagall

32. Cracka Ass Cracka 5.11d (T) ★★

Climbs the crack just to the right of Schizophrenic Boulevard. From the ledge head up and then out the roof crack. Pulling the lip is the crux but once on the headwall trend left and finish on the Smokin' Guns anchors. *SR.*

FA: Aaron Collins

33. Smokin' Guns 5.12a ★★★★

Climbs the impressive roof near the back of the Acropolis. Start up the slick rock onto the ledge then make a few delicate moves up to the first bolt. From there enjoy big moves on big holds through the roof to the lip, where a few cruxy moves will get you onto the headwall. 6 bolts (including 4 fixed draws).

FA: Jim Steagall, Eric Hanson

34. Fish Head 5.13c/d ★

Starts off the top of the dam; make your way up and left to the first bolt. A strong, tricky sequence follows through the bulge. After pulling the overhang follow the crack to the anchors. 5 bolts, stick clip recommended.

> *Originally established in 1993 by Chris Raypole and Manny Rangel. Fish Head was an open project for thirteen years until it finally saw a first ascent by Brett Monik. In 2025, with permission from the first ascensionist, all of the flexing holds that had been epoxied on were removed and it saw its first ascent free of any glue.*

FA: Brett Monik '06   FFA: Richie Winter '25

35. Flakes of Wrath 5.11b ★★

Starts off the top of the dam. Climb up the overhang (big moves, big holds!) and into the delicate crux before the anchors. 4 bolts.

FA: Dave Sobocan, Jim Steagall

36. Shark Attack 5.12b ★★

Just to the right of Flakes of Wrath above a large boulder. The boulder can be used to clip the first bolt but beware -- any big falls would likely result in smashing into it. A short, stout overhang with positive holds all the way. 3 bolts.

FA: Ken Mills

SOUTH SIDE OF THE ACROPOLIS

☀ ALL DAY SHADE

To get to routes #37-#44 scramble up the dam and continue upstream for a few hundred yards until it opens up to the right. Follow a trail and handlines up the scree slope and broken ledges.

37. Friendly Fire 5.13a ★★★★

A technical, thin face down low into an ever-steepening wall up high. Compression, crimps and possibly the best kneebar in central Arizona will get you through the crux. 11 bolts.

FA: Richie Winter, Charlie Brown

38. Karma Farmer 5.12d ★★★★

Start up lower angle loose rock onto a shield of solid stone. Fun movement up crimps and sidepulls to anchors below the roof. 8 bolts.

FA: Richie Winter, Charlie Brown

39. Friendly Farmer 13a ★★★★

An extension of Karma Farmer. Climb up the original line. To reduce drag higher up, don't clip the anchors of Karma Farmer; option to clip the last bolt with a runner or skip clipping it altogether as well. Follow the bolt line that cuts left out the roof on steep and pumpy underclings. Pull out the roof and onto Friendly Fire. Shares the last bolt and anchors with Friendly Fire.

FA: Richie Winter, Charlie Brown

40. CLOSED PROJECT

An extension of Karma Farmer.

41. Slap and Tickle 5.10d ★★★★

P1 Climb up into steep, exposed bombay chimney that looks harder than it is until the final moves out right to the anchor. 6 bolts.

P2 Far less trafficked than the first pitch so be cautious of suspect rock. Continue up the face above the chimney. Bolted, open-book crack climbing. Belay from the comfortable ledge.

P3 A scarcely bolted scramble gets you to the very top of the formation. Easily linked with the second pitch.

FA: Manny Rangel

42. Black and Tan 5.11b/c ★★

Climb up the thin face on flexing crimps, sticking to the left side of the arete for most of the route. At the final bolt move over to the right side of the arete and continue up to the anchors. Shares anchors with P1 of Slap and Tickle. 8 bolts.

FA: Manny Rangel

43. Unnamed Chimney 5.6 (T)

Obvious chimney just behind Jester. Clip one bolt (and an old piton if you wish) down low and chimney up the gap as it widens and finish on top of the formation. Rap via Jester. *SR.*

FA: Don O'Kelley, Kent Brock

44. Jester 5.10d

Follows a vertical seam to the top of the lone pillar. 9 bolts.

FA: Mike Thompson, Mark Harris

45. The Mangler 5.11b ★★

Climbs the west facing arete at the top of the dam, just past the scree gulley. A reachy crux down low leads to easier climbing at the top. 9 bolts.

FA: Manny Rangel

46. Diaper Rash 5.10a

Climbs the face just to the right of The Mangler. Thin, techy, and slightly runout. 5 bolts.

FA: Mark Harris, Jay Clark, Eric Agaciewski

47. US Senators are Space Aliens 5.11a

On the right side of the scree gulley. Climb to the left of the bolt line for the first two bolts. A cruxy third bolt leads to easier, but not necessarily trivial, climbing over the bulge to the anchors. 6 bolts, stick clip recommended.

FA: Mark Harris, Jay Clark, Eric Agaciewski

48. Unfinished Business 5.12b/c ★★★

A high first bolt leads to a crux coming out the roof. Pull hard on pockets and crimps until a rest at the fourth bolt. Easier but still thoughtful climbing to the anchors. 5 bolts, including one fixed draw, stick clip recommended.

FA: Kevin Benson, Cole Benson

49. Marceline 5.12 PG-13 (T) ★★★

An adventerous three pitch climb that starts off the top of the dam. Requires at least a 60m rope.

P1 (5.12a/b) Off the top of the dam start into a crimpy boulder problem to access the crack system. Follow the finger crack to the slab. Then traverse left under the roof to gain access to a wide hand crack out the roof. After the roof continue up the easier but slightly chossy crack to a bolted anchor.

P2 (5.8) PG-13 Traverse to the right past a few bolts and some old tat.

P3 (5.8) Easy off-width to a ledge. Continue up and over a bulge into a thin crack. Scramble up to the base of P3 of The Trident.

To descend rap the first two pitches of The Trident.

FA: Richie Winter

50. The Woo 5.12d ★★★

A mixed line that starts the same as for Marceline. Follow the finger crack and head straight out the roof.

FA: Richie Winter

51. KingFisher 5.14a ★★★

Climbs the bulge, starting just below the dam. Two defined boulder problems seperated by a juggy but overhanging rest. 4 bolts

FA: Richie Winter

52. Duck and Cover 5.11c

Start up the river polished rock, through the bulge, and onto the face above. 6 bolts.

FA: Ken Mills, Matt Krise

53. Double Trouble 5.8 (T) ★★

The classic Atlantis slick start leads into a double crack feature that runs between Duck and Cover and Shoot First Ask Later. At the top, step right to use the anchors for Shoot First Ask Later. *SR.*

FA: Scott Duemler

54. Shoot First Ask Later 5.12a ★★★

Start up the slick, vertical face on good holds to a ledge. From there head into the slightly overhanging crux -- thin holds to a committing move to a jug. Continue up easier terrain to the anchors. Wall to the left of the crack is off. 8 bolts.

FA: Jim Steagall, Dave Sobocan

55. Grumpy After Eight 5.10a ★★★

Head up the water polished rock, broken up by a few good ledges, for four bolts then power up the slightly overhanging wall. 9 bolts.

FA: Jim Steagall, Eric Hanson

56. First Born 5.8 ★★★

Start up the dihedral toward the obvious chimney. Shimmy your way up; once you make it out follow jugs to the top. 8 bolts.

FA: Scott Duemler

57. Double Exposure 5.11b

Shares the start with First Born, but instead of heading toward the chimney cut right toward the dihedral. Enjoy fun, stemmy movement through the dihedral before pulling the roof at the top. Once you've gained the sloping ledge, traverse left and head up the bolt line that skirts the looming roof overhead. Known for some serious drag at the top, be prepared to rap off the line instead of lowering. 11 bolts.

FA: Scott Duemler

58. Direct Exposure 5.12a ★★★★

A direct start and direct finish to Double Exposure. Just outside of the dihedral clip a low first bolt (reach down and back clean this bolt after clipping the second to reduce drag). Move up and right at the second bolt and gain the sloping ledge. Take advantage of the quick rest if you'd like before heading into the first crux: three bolts of technical movement on crimps until you reach the sloping edge. The next three bolts through the dihedral are shared with Double Exposure. Pull out the right side of the first roof at the top of the dihedral (once you've pulled the roof unclip the chain draw to reduce drag). Take the opportunity for another quick rest before heading into the final crux, making your way up the ever-steepening wall into the final roof. 14 bolts.

FA: Charlie Brown, Cas Sundell

59. Overbearing Underminer 5.11c ★★★

A hard, slopey boulder problem off the ground leads to easier terrain for a few bolts. As the angle steepens you'll encounter a fixed draw; high clip to protect the crux. Pull through the balancey crux on incut crimps to gain a slabby rest. From there the difficulty lessens as you head up vertical to off-vert terrain. At the large horizonal split trend to the right and head up the small, flaring chimney to the anchors. 12 bolts.

FA: Fred AmRhein, Chris Remsburg

60. KGB 5.10b ★★

Start up the thin face to a cruxy roof near the top. Pull the roof and climb the runout face to the top. Be careful not to wander onto Giggling Marlin after the roof. 7 bolts.

FA: Bill Burns, Gary Burns, Ken Mills

61. Giggling Marlin 5.9 ★★★

Start off the large boulder. A high first bolt leads to fun face climbing with a good variety of movement and holds that keep it interesting all the way to the anchors. 8 bolts.

FA: Bill Burns, Gary Burns

62. Myrmidon 5.10b ★★★★

Start off the same boulder as for Giggling Marlin. Climb straight through the low crux out the bulge and onto the slabby face above. Jugs take you out the roof and onto another lower angle section before the final steep headwall. Race to the chains before the pump sets in! 13 bolts.

FA: Charlie Brown, Ben Ramsey, Cas Sundell

63. Bunny Slope 5.10a ★★★

Start up the vertical face and pull the small, cruxy roof on incut holds. Head up the lower angle wall to another vertical section and make your way through the second crux, pulling over a bulge, before heading up into the chimney. 12 bolts.

FA: Brett Clark

SOUTH SIDE

☀ MORNING SHADE

Located on the south side of the wash, just across the way from the Kitty Pool. Although the South Side gets early morning shade, the sun hits it before noon, so even in the winter you can plan on warmer rock.

64. Sir Charles 5.10a ★★★

Just outside The Acropolis. Start up the flaring crack past two bolts and onto a large ledge. Clip a high bolt and head up the vertical face on good but sometimes crimpy holds. 7 bolts.

FA: Mike Thompson, Carmen Bastek

65. Hide and Seek 5.7 (T) ★

Climb the long, obvious crack to the right of Sir Charles. A variety of fun, three-dimensional movement will get you to the top as the crack gradually widens. *SR, double 4, 5, optional 6.* Bolted anchor.

FA: Scott Duemler

66. Ali Cat 5.7 ★★★★

Just to the right of Hide and Seek. Climb the tall, broken pillar on rock that's much better than it may look. Dead vertical but every hold is a jug. 9 bolts.

FA: Scott Duemler, Aaron Collins

67. The Phoenix 5.9 ★★

Although slightly shorter, reminiscent of The Trident and a fantastic option if the classic Atlantis multipitch has a long line on it. Starts up and around the corner from Ali Cat. Scramble up past a cat claw to a roomy ledge to begin P1, or clip the first two bolts of Ali Cat before transitioning over to the ledge (not recommended, as Ali Cat is heavily trafficked).

P1 (5.7) Climb the broken face past one large ledge to the anchors. 5 bolts.

P2 (5.9) Starts up a steeper face on jugs before easing into a massive ledge. 5 bolts.

P3 (5.9) Head out the roof on large holds. 5 bolts.

Rap each pitch to descend.

FA: Aaron Collins, Scott Duemler, A. Wehn, S. Rutherford

68. Rachel's Route 5.10a ★★★

Just up and around the corner from pitch one of The Trident. A fun, pocketed face leads to a ledge. High clip the fixed draw and continue up the sustained face to a high crux. 12 bolts, including one fixed draw.

FA: Scott Duemler, Alexis Ely

69. Mondo Freako 5.7 ★

Starts off the small ledge with the tree. Short, pocketed face. 3 bolts.

FA: Chad Cooper

70. The Trident 5.9 ★★★

The most trafficked multipitch in Atlantis by far. Originally done on gear and now bolted from top to bottom, The Trident is a great multipitch to cut your teeth on (as long as you have a good head on your shoulders; some of bolts can feel pretty spaced out where the climbing is easy) and follows good holds all the way.

P1 (5.7) Start up Mondo Freako, clip a draw at the anchors, and continue up for another twenty or so feet to anchor in an alcove. Take care not to send any large rocks toward your belayer as you approach the anchor. 5 bolts.

P2 (5.8) Climb the broken face to an anchor on top of the pillar. 8 bolts (and one old piton, so count on 9 draws if you want to clip that).

P3 (5.9) From the P2 anchors make your way across the bushy ledge and start up slightly over vertical wall with a high first bolt. Follows the broken seam. The hardest bit is down low, and as the angle lets off

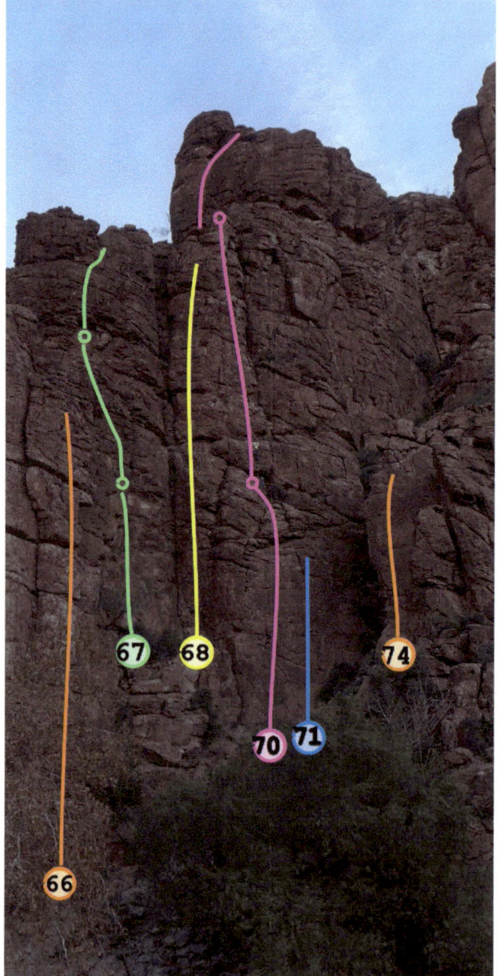

the bolts get further apart. 4 bolts.

From the summit, you can descend or walk a short ways to the base of Poseidon's Throne and continue the adventure upwards.

To descend, either walk off the back side along an established trail or rap the three pitches. Keep in mind that, being a trafficked route, it's generally better to walk off, especially on a weekend. If you do choose to rappel be courteous of parties coming up.

FKA: Matt Johnson, Michael Genovese, Troy Dixon

71. G-String 5.7 ★

Just right of Mondo Freako. Climb a similar low angle, short, pocketed face. 3 bolts.

FA: Marilyn Geninatti, Jim Anglin

72. See You Try, See You Fail Direct Start 5.11a ★★

Located on the backside of the feature slightly up the hill from Mondo Freako. The better of the two lines on the short, slightly overhanging face. Small holds get you through the crux and fun jugs get you to the anchor. 6 bolts.

FA: Chad Cooper

73. See You Try, See You Fail 5.10d ★

The right bolt line of the two on the backside of the feature uphill from Mondo Freako. Climb huge pockets to a high first bolt, then continue up the left side of the arete before cutting left and traversing along the seam. Shares the last two bolts with the 5.11. 5 bolts.

FA: Chad Cooper

74. Mickey Mouse 5.9 ★★

On the north facing side of the feature uphill from Mondo Freako. Start up a broken section to a ledge then continue up the clean face, occasionally utilizing the arete. 6 bolts.

FA: Chad Cooper, Briana Broderick

Routes #75-#77 are located on a separate outcropping of rock downstream from the main South Side area, toward the right side of the trailhead for Funny Farm. Look for a pillar with a large anchor attached to it for the wire supporting the old water pipe.

75. Gluten Intolerance 5.10a ★

Climbs the front face of the lone pillar. Scramble up onto a ledge to belay. Clip a high first bolt and head up the steep face. A sustained route with a variety of holds. 4 bolts.

FA: Jacob Marcy, Jackson Sims Myers, Ben Ramsey

76. Coping Mechanism 5.9 ★

On the west-facing side of the lone pillar. A short but fun route. Stem up the dihedral to a jug rail just below the roof. The difficulty eases once past the upper bulge. 5 bolts.

FA: Tyler Collins, Michael Genovese

77. Edge of Tears 5.6 ★

Right of Coping Mechanism and up the scree slope. A short, pocketed face. Tricky for the first half but eases off the closer you get to the anchors. 4 bolts.

FA: Scott Duemler, Michael Genovese

THE FUNNY FARM

☀ MORNING SHADE

The Funny Farm is located on the cliff band across the canyon from and level with the main parking area. From the main Atlantis area, hike downstream about 30 yards. To your left will be a clear, steep trail marked with a cairn.

Shaded in the morning but as the afternoon ticks on expect more and more sun.

78. Jesus is Real 5.11 ★★★★

A continuous, pumpy sequence leads to a jug at the fourth bolt ("If you can't wrap your head around Jesus, you can at least wrap your hand over the jug below the fourth bolt."). Continue up a few more powerful moves on slightly overhanging terrain to a ledge (better known as The Smoking Lounge) that provides a full no-hands rest. Once you're ready to keep moving, traverse left into the crack and head up less powerful but more technical terrain to the anchors.

FA: Aaron Peterson, Scott Duemler, Michael Genovese

79. Little Lost Lion 5.9 (T) ★★★

The corner crack just to the right of Jesus is Real. Make your way up the steep crack utilizing jams, stems, and crimps. You even get a taste of offwidth! *SR, 4.*

FA: Ryan Myers, Clay Lippincott, Scott Duemler

80. Rocket Man 5.11a/b ★★

A tricky start leads to a burly roof. Pull hard through the roof then transition onto the delicate off-vertical face with great friction. 12 bolts, including 2 fixed draws.

FA: Clay Lippincott

81. Pole Dancing Dragons 5.8 ★★

The left of the two lines on the lower angle face around the corner from Rocket Man.

P1 (5.8) Follows the featured, frictiony face. Trend left as you head up to utilize the arete. If intending to do both pitches of this route, throw a draw on the anchor and head up another five feet to a nice belay ledge with a separate anchor. Use this anchor to bring up your second. 10 bolts.

P2 (5.8) Easier climbing off the ledge leads to a short, steeper section. Pull onto the sloping ramp and finish with trickier climbing. 8 bolts.

Descend in two rappels.

FA: Clay Lippincott, David Jacobs, Ryan Myers, Tyler Eglen

82. Seats of Evil 5.8 ★★

The right of the two lines on the lower angle face around the corner from Rocket Man. Fun face climbing up a well-featured wall.

FA: Clay Lippincott, David Jacobs, Ryan Myers, Tyler Eglen

83. The Corral of Voices 5.8 (T) ★★★

Follows the corner crack system to the right of Seats of Evil.

P1 (5.7) Cruise up the corner system to bolted anchors. The trickiest bit is down low.

P2 (5.8) Finger, hand, and fist jams lead to a sweet chimney. Bolted anchors.

SR, optional 4.

Recommended to descend in two rappels. It is possible to get down in one with a 70m rope but it is a full 35m rap. Tie knots in your rope and aim for the top of the large boulder at the start of P1.

There is an optional, much more adventurous third pitch that requires a bit of commitment as there's no anchor, a few portable holds, and a bit of gardening at the top. Continue up the crack until you reach the top of the Funny Farm. Descend via Poseidon's Throne.

FA: Unknown

84. First Dance 5.10c/d ★

A stout line up a short, steep wall. Start up an easy boulder to the first bolt on the overhanging face. Fire up through the boulder problem at the bottom, clipping the bolts on your left. Take care not to get sucked too far right into the crack between the first and second bolts. 7 bolts.

FA: Stephen Baklund, Clay Lippincott, Tyler Eglen, David Jacobs, Ryan Myers

85. Spaceball 5.7 (T)

On the west-facing wall around the corner from First Dance. A short route that leads to a prominent ledge. Climb this route if you've done every other trad line in the canyon and you're trying to tick them all. Difficult to find protection in the lower half. Very poor rock quality (to the point where some of it may never be clean no matter how trafficked, and some dangerous blocks still remain). Mediocre climbing combined with some serious safety issues. *0.5-3.*

FA: Tyler Egln, Clay Lippincott, David Jacobs, Ryan Myers

86. Curley the Spandex Alien 5.11 ★

A technical start leads to a big move at the roof. Once you've made your way over the lip, cruise to the anchors. Be mindful of softer rock right below the roof and don't get tricked into the offwidth to the left. 13 bolts.

FA: Justine Poole, Clay Lippincott

87. Decompressing the Delusions ★
Shares the first three bolts with Serious Enthusiasm. Once you reach the big ledge, cut left onto the west-facing wall. Continue up the left-leaning bolt line to the anchors. 13 bolts.

FA: Tyler Eglen

88. Especial 5.7 (T) ★
Follows the large crack to the left of Serious Enthusiasm. Beware sections of loose rock, especially on the ledge three quarters of the way up. *0.5-4, nuts.* There is no designated anchor for this route. To descend either scramble to the anchors on Serious Enthusiasm or walk off.

FA: Ryan Myers, David Jacobs, Clay Lippincott, Tyler Eglen

89. Serious Enthusiasm 5.8 ★★★
Good climbing on positive holds up the steep wall. Shares the first three bolts with Decompressing the Delusions; once you reach the big ledge continue straight up. A full 35m pitch so a 70m rope is a requirement. 15 bolts.

FA: Ryan Myers, David Jacobs, Clay Lippincott, Tyler Eglen

LOWER ATLANTIS

MORNING SHADE

Located around 100 yards downstream from the main Atlantis area, Lower Atlantis is a small alcove with a decent range of routes that stays shaded all day.

90. Mansplaining 5.11c ★★★
Clip a high first bolt from the boulder before starting. Climbs a vertical, delicate face through crimps and incut sidepulls to a series of overhangs split by a flaring crack. Builds quite a pump for how short it is, but this steep little climb is the gem of the wall. 8 bolts.

FA: Cas Sundell, Charlie Brown

91. Rage Bait 5.10b ★★★
Technical face climbing on crimps leads to a series of fun, steep sidepulls and liebacks and culminates in a heartbreaking overhang at the top. The route climbs the face; if you decide to climb into the obviously loose chimney to the left at the beginning, that's on you. 6 bolts.

FA: Cas Sundell, Charlie Brown

92. Milwaukee Menorah 5.9 ★★★
Cruise up well-protected climbing through jugs to a few thought-provoking, powerful moves at the top. 7 bolts.

FA: Cas Sundell, Charlie Brown

93. Cherry Jubilee 5.7 ★★★

Climbs the arete on big, positive holds the whole way up. 6 bolts.

FA: Chase Warren, Dave Gunn, Quentin George

94. Silent Partner 5.8 ★★

The only route in Lower Atlantis that ever sees sunlight, and only in the afternoon. Climbs a vertical face with a low crux. Pull through that and you're rewarded with fun, juggy climbing for the rest of the route. 6 bolts.

FA: Unknown

LITTLE ENGLAND WALL

An expansive east-facing wall that is shaded by noon and stays that way the rest of the day. Home to some of the very first ascents in the canyon, climbers have been coming here since the early seventies to plug gear into the wall. Staying true to its history, most of the routes are traditional and tend be a little more adventurous than the sport lines in nearby Atlantis.

GETTING THERE

From the pull out just after the tunnel on US-60, hike down into the canyon via the Atlantis trail, head upstream, and scramble up the dam. From the top of the dam walk a few hundred feet until a fairly obvious trail to your right appears near some old cables. Approximately ten minutes from the main Atlantis area.

1. Brutus: Ides of March 5.5 (T) ★

On the south side of the southwest pinnacle in the group of towers above the Little England Wall. Can be approached from the main Little England trail or from the Funny Farm. Climbs the obvious wide, broken crack in the notch between the southwest and southeast pinnacle. .3-6, nuts. Rap off.

FA: Jon Biemer, Frank Hill, Ed Sampson

2. Caesar 5.3 (T) ★

Climb the face on the lower pinnacle near Brutus, using small to medium pro in the broken cracks. *.3-2, nuts.* Rap off.

FA: Jon Biemer, Frank Hill, Ed Sampson

3. The Bishop: Changeover Route 5.9 (T) ★

From the Little England Wall head 200 yards east and uphill.

P1 Follows a crack on the south side of the pinnacle to a comfy belay ledge.

P2 Continue up the crack as it winds around the east side to the top of the pillar.

SR. Rap off.

PHOTO: BEN ALBRECHT

FA: Kent Brock, Don O'Kelley

4. Palace of Westminster 5.10a ★★★

From the Little England Wall branch off left on a faint trail toward a lone pinnacle. Starting on the left side of the formation, head up low fourth class to the first bolt then make your way up the continuous face on good edges. 12 bolts.

FA: Michael Wolansky, Ben Albrecht, Nick Schostack, Tyler Collins, Michael Genovese

5. The Shard of Glass 5.7 (T) ★★

From the Little England Walll branch off left on the same trail that leads toward Palace of Westminster and continue up the gully. About thirty feet past The Gherkin is the base of The Shard of Glass.

P1 Just past the tree start up the finger crack -- there's good gear and good feet -- and continue up to the bulge. From here you have the option to head up the dirty hand crack, or cut left on good holds (but with no pro) and make a few moves up to a ledge where the crack ends. From the ledge head toward the horizontal chimney staircase and, using a combination of face climbing, walking, and straddling, make your way across the separated flake until you can make the traverse to the anchors. Bolted anchor.

P2 Around the corner from the anchors is a chimney. Head up the chimney to the top. Gear anchor.

.3-6, nuts.

To descend, use fixed rap gear on the east side of the summit. 70m rope necessary.

FA: Ben Albrecht, Phoenix Parker

6. The Gherkin 5.7 (T) ★★

From the Little England Wall branch off left and head up toward a tree and spire with tat on the top. Climbs a wide crack with a featured face to either side and finishes with some unlikely chimney moves. *.2-6.*

FA: Ben Albrecht

7. Athletic Supporter 5.7 A3 (T) ★

Hike up the gulley to a north-facing wall with a thin crack above the 3 bolt pillar. Aid a thin crack through two overhangs to a bolted anchor.

FA: Bill Rickard, Mike Kozma

8. A-1 Steak Sauce 5.11a ★

From the Little England Wall cut left. Climbs the bolted face on a standalone pillar. 3 bolts.

FA: Bill Rickard, Mike Kozma

9. Henry VIII 5.6 (T) ★★

Far left end of the Little England Wall. Follows the right-facing dihedral to bolted anchors. *SR.*

FA: Don O'Kelley, Kent Brock

10. Charles II 5.6 (T) ★

Thirty feet to the right of Henry VIII. Follows the right-facing dihedral to bolted anchors. *SR.*

FA: Don O'Kelley, Kent Brock

11. Anne of a Thousand Days 5.7 (T) ★★

Start the same as for Charles II. Follow the right-facing dihedral until you can cut off into cracks to the right. When the crack breaks into three, follow the rightmost crack to bolted anchors at the top. A 70m rope will get you down but may require some easy downclimbing; some prefer to bring a second rope for the descent. *SR.*

FA: Don O'Kelley, Kent Brock

12. Bloody Mary 5.7 ★★★

To the right of Anne of a Thousand Days.

P1 (5.7) Begin below a small roof in the alcove. Once above the roof, trend to the left as you head for the anchors. 11 bolts.

P2 (5.7+) Continue up the face on fun holds. 7 bolts.

Can be done as one 18 bolt pitch. Descend in two rappels.

FA: Tyler Collins, Ben Albrecht

13. West Minster Abbey 5.7 (T) ★★

Starts roughly twenty feet to the right of the right-facing dihedral.

P1 Follow the obvious vertical crack to a ledge near the top. Expect poor protection down low but know that it gets better the higher you get.

P2 Continue following the crack to the top.

To descend, rap off the same bolted anchor as for Henry VIII. *SR.*

FA: Don O'Kelley, Kent Brock

14. The Thames 5.9 ★★★

Twenty feet to the left of Big Ben, look for a tan hanger on a high first bolt.

P1 Easy climbing to the first bolt then continue up the face -- it looks harder than it is. After the fifth bolt traverse right about 20 feet to a bolt under the roof. Extend the two bolts on the traverse to save yourself the drag. Pull over the cruxy roof on solid rails then trend slightly left and head up to the anchors on a large ledge. 9 bolts.

P2 Head straight up from the ledge before eventually trending slightly left toward a chossy roof. Under the roof cut right toward a bolt just above. Solid rock above the roof to the anchors. If you'd like to top out, you can climb above the anchors to another set on top. 9 bolts.

FA: Tyler Collins, Ben Albrecht

15. Big Ben 5.7 (T) ★★

Starts in a corner with a somewhat built out belay area next to a tree.

P1 Start up the face next to the corner into a crack with several ledges. Continue up the crack to a ledge near the top. Single bolt belay; save some smaller cams for your anchor.

P2 (PG-13) Continue up the crack. As it widens, your options for gear lessens. Two bolt anchor.

.5-6, nuts.

To descend, rap the two bolt anchor at the top of Henry VIII or rap the second pitch. To avoid rapping off the single bolt at the top of P1 you can swing about 15 feet to the left and use the P1 anchors of The Thames.

FA: Don O'Kelley, Kent Brock

16. London Tower 5.7 (T) ★★

Starts 40 feet to the right of Big Ben.

P1 Start up a wide crack and continue up until you gain access to another crack to the left. Follow that crack up and into a chimney behind a flake.

P2 Climb the chimney to the top of the flake then continue up a crack and the face to a small ledge.

P3 Head up and cut left into the Big Ben crack and follow it to the top.

.5-6, nuts.

To descend, rap the two bolt anchor at the top of Henry VIII.

FA: Don O'Kelley, Kent Brock

17. Stonehenge 5.6 (T) ★

P1 Start the same as for London Tower, up the wide crack and chimney before following crack right to a ledge.

P2 Follow the crack to the top.

.3-5, nuts.

FA: Jim Hatfield and class

18. The Mighty Barge 5.10b ★

Climbs the Smokestack Pinnacle at the north end of the Little England Wall. Originally done all on gear, the second party bolted the first pitch. Most people only climb the first pitch, which can be done entirely without gear.

P1 Climb up the face to a ledge and the top of the pinnacle. 10 bolts.

P2 Continue up the face, past broken cracks, to the top. *.3-3.*

FA: Mark Harris, John Save, Mike Pence

19. Zeus 5.10d ★★★

Just around the corner from the Smokestack Pinnacle. Easily accessed from the Little England trail or from walking off the backside of The Trident.

A mixed route that follows the obvious lighting bolt crack. Start up the crack for around forty feet -- the trad section climbs around 5.9 -- to gain access to the cruxy, bolted face that continues to get harder and harder as time wanes on. *8 bolts, SR, 4, optional 5.*

FA: Michael Gladkin, Manny Rangel, Matt Johnson

20. Dirty Corner 5.6

Low angle dihedral. And, as the name suggests, quite dirty and rarely climbed. *.5-3.*

FA: Unknown

21. Unknown Face (AKA G.P. Route) 5.9 ★★

To the right of Zeus, climb the clean face on positive edges through some fairly runout sections. Can be done as a single pitch, but more commonly done as a variation to P1 of Poseidon's Throne. 8 bolts.

FA: Unknown

22. Poseidon's Throne 5.10c ★★★

Easily accessed via the Little England trail, but is more commonly done as a linkup with The Trident and can be accessed from walking off the backside of the three pitch route.

P1 (5.6) Start up the handcrack on the right side of the bolted face, then transition out onto an exposed arete with big holds and even bigger views. *4 bolts, .75-3.*

An excellent variation to P1 is the G.P. Route (5.9), which ends on the same ledge.

A less excellent variation to P1 is Textbook (5.6), to the left of the bolted face.

P2 (5.10c) From the huge ledge, start up the face (right hand in the crack, left hand on the face) and follow the winding bolt line to the top. In the middle, be mindful of staying exactly on route to remain on solid rock. 9 bolts.

To descend, rap both pitches.

FA: Matt Johnson

23. Textbook 5.4

Low angle dihedral on the west side of the formation. *.3-2.*

FA: Jon Biemer

QUEEN SCEPTER

Queen Scepter is an impressive free-standing tower upstream from Atlantis, easily recognizable by the series of roofs on its west face.

GETTING THERE

From Superior, take US-60 east for three miles and park at the third pull off on the south side of the road (same as for The Pond). Scramble down into the creek on the southwest side of the lot and head uphill to gain a trail that cuts across the side of the canyon. Hike west along the well defined trail for 0.2 miles toward the obvious formation.

Another option is to park at the second pull off on the south side of the road (by the decommissioned monument), drop down into the creek, scramble up the scree across the creek, and head west on the same trail toward the tower. While this option does technically require less hiking, it's arguably more difficult, as you'll have to scramble up the loose scree for quite a ways to reach the trail.

1. Queen of Hearts 5.12c ★★

Left-most line on the west side of the formation. Climb up the easier (but not necessarily easy) face to the series of cruxy, small roofs. 15 bolts.

FA: Jim Steagall, Deidre Burton

2. Queen Scepter 5.12a ★★★

Climbs up the center of the west face. Start up the vertical face to the series of roof and bulges. While the technical crux may be short-lived, the route remains overhanging almost the entire way, making for a pumpy ascent. 15 bolts.

FA: Jim Steagall, Ken Mills, Eric Hanson

3. King of Fools 5.11d ★★

Lone route on the south side of the formation. Climb up the face and through a cruxy bulge on the southeast arete. Once you pull onto the lower angle face above the bulge, continue up thin holds to the anchors. Stepping out onto the ramp leading to Whistling Idiot is cheating. 10 bolts.

FA:Jim Steagall, Ken Mills

4. Whistling Idiot 5.10b ★

Left-most line on the east side of the formation. Scramble up to a pair of belay bolts and then head up on big holds. 4 bolts.

FA: Jim Steagall, Ken Mills

5. Unnamed Crack 5.8 (T)

Follows the crack to the right of Whistling Idiot. *SR.* Rap off on the anchors of Whistling Idiot.

FA: Kent Brock, Don O'Kelley

GETTING THERE

From Superior, take US-60 east for three miles to the third pull out on the right. It is the only pull out with a large rock mound in the middle of it, so it's easy to be sure you're at the right one.

From Globe, take US-60 west for 21 miles.
(33.30846, 111.07089)

From the pull out, walk east up canyon alongside the highway until you reach the bridge. Take the trail down and underneath the bridge to avoid having to dash across the roadway. Once you're on the other side of the highway, trend up and right across the boulders to the east side of the creek, where you'll eventually encounter a small pool with a tree at the edge. Look for rebar rungs on the wall behind the tree, these make the traverse around the edge of the pool much easier. Once on the other side of the pool, continue to follow the rebar rungs up the fourth class terrain.

At the top, you should be able to see the eponymous pond and the start of a few different routes -- most noticably being the sweeping overhanging wall with area test piece Desert Devil. There is a web of trail systems to work your way back across to the west side of the creek; they'll all more or less get you to the same place, so don't stress too much about which one to take.

THE POND

The Pond is, understandably, one of the most popular destinations in the canyon. Not only does it boast some of the more notorious hard routes Queen Creek Canyon has to offer, but it is home to a multitude of fun moderates, making it a great place to spend the day.

The majority of the crag is south facing and generally stays very warm; you'll find the best conditions here on especially chilly or overcast days.

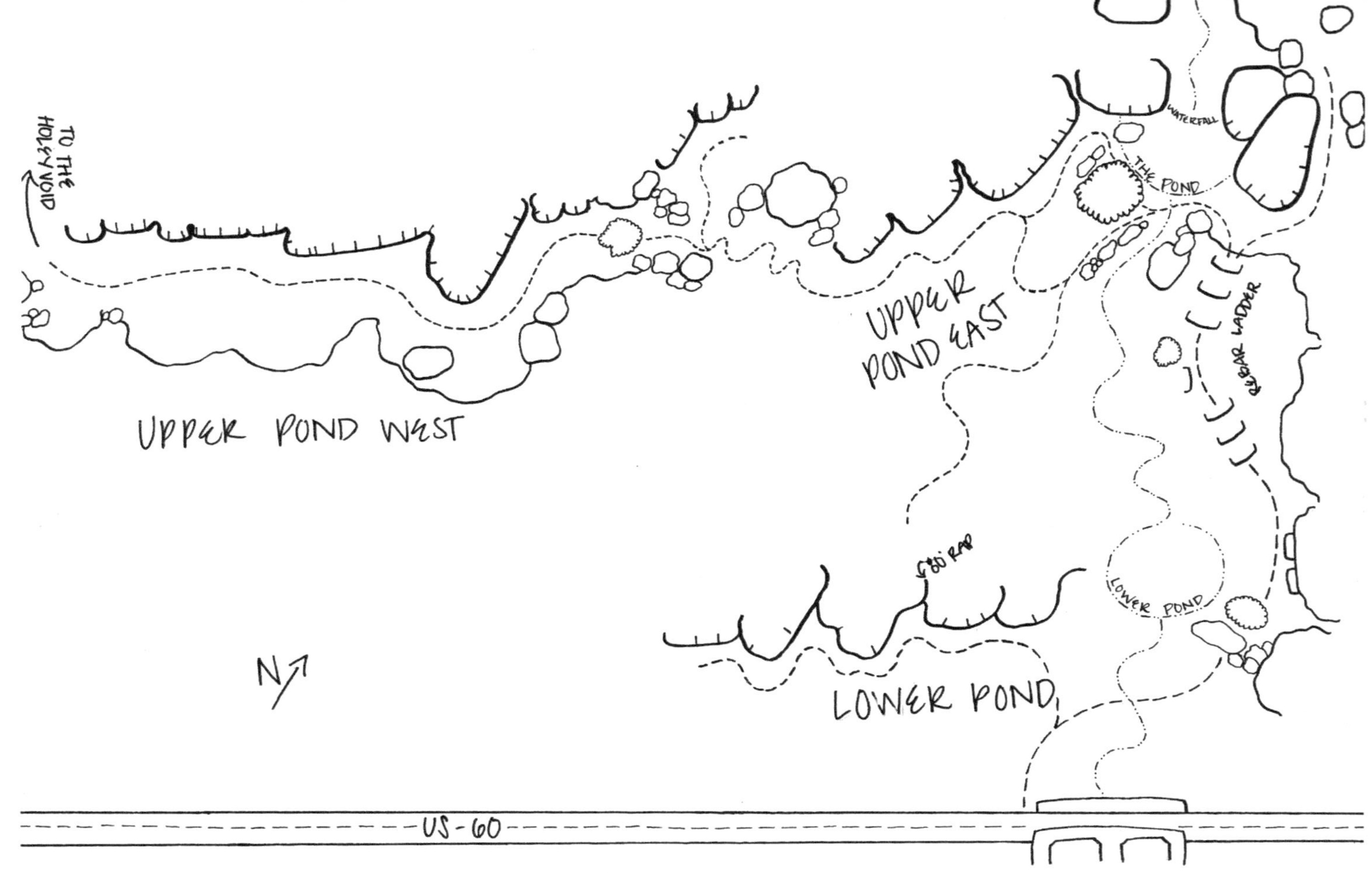
TO THE HOLEY VOID
UPPER POND WEST
UPPER POND EAST
WATERFALL
THE POND
REBAR LADDER
80' RAP
LOWER POND
LOWER POND
N
US-60

THE HOLEY VOID

☀ MORNING SHADE

The Holey Void is the furthest left area at The Pond. From the top of the rebar ladder, make your way across to the west side of the creek and follow the trail that traverses along the cliff. Continue on the trail until it seems to end (if you've reached a substantial ocotillo at the end of a ledge you've gone just a few steps too far). From there scramble up easy second or third class for a few feet and you'll find that the trail forges on. From the top of the scramble it's only around a hundred feet before you encounter the first routes in The Holey Void.

Routes #1 - #11 are on the west side of a small drainage/waterfall, routes #12 - #21 are on the east.

1. Beyond the Void 5.10a ★

On the west side of the small drainage continue on the trail; when it rounds the corner, hike uphill until it plateaus. The route is on a separate pillar at the top of the hill. Short, pocketed face. 5 bolts.

FA: Greg Opland, Mike Kaczocha, Pat Metz

2. Fleshy Headed Mutant 5.10c ★

On the west side of the small drainage, around the corner. Thin face. 5 bolts.

FA: Eric Ebele, John Duboe

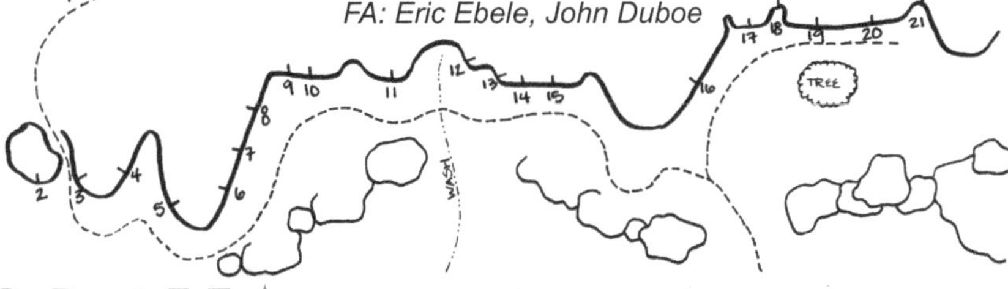

3. Deet 5.7 ★

Follows a clean, three bolt face to anchors. The feet are trickier than the hands! 3 bolts.

FA: Eric Ebele, Dawn Thompson

4. Cleansing 5.11b ★

Short face located in a small corridor just around the corner from the small drainage. Okay climbing, but stays shady longer than some other routes.

FA: Frank Veers, Richard Horst

5. Princess Jordini and Her Magic Flute 5.5 ★

A heavily pocketed, off vertical face with a short runout. 3 bolts.

FA: Eric Ebele, John Duboe

6. Nothing But Air 5.11d ★★

Furthest left on the east facing wall just past the drainage. A bouldery start leads to thin face. 5 bolts.

FA: Fred AmRhein, Michelle AmRhein

7. Is Nothing Sacred 5.11c ★★

On the east facing wall just past the drainage. Climb up thin pockets between a thin crack and right leaning seam to a steep wall with more pockets. 5 bolts.

FA: Fred AmRhein, Michelle AmRhein

8. Nothing's There 5.12a ★★

The right-most route on the east facing wall just past the drainage. Start up and right along the seam, utilizing a pod-like feature. Eventually, cross back to the left and continue to the anchors. 6 bolts.

FA: Fred AmRhein, Michelle AmRhein

9. Next To Nothing 5.7 ★

A short, thought-provoking route. After the second bolt, the climbing eases into easier-to-read slab. 4 bolts.

FA: Scott Aldinger, Lisa Schmitz

10. Nothing Box 5.6

Barely to the right of Next To Nothing. Climb pockets along the seam to anchors shared with Next To Nothing. 4 bolts.

FA: Unknown

11. Nothing To It 5.10c ★

Starts off a small ledge by a large boulder. A short, but pumpy, slightly overhanging face. 5 bolts.

FA: Scott Aldinger, Fred AmRhein, Lisa Schmitz

12. Nothing Becomes Her 5.9 ★

Climbs the thin column immediately to the right of the small waterfall. Uses the odd water-polished hold on the face and more textured holds on the arete. 5 bolts.

FA: Sandy Draus, Lisa Schmitz

13. Nothing Shocking 5.8 ★★

Climbs the arete to the right of Nothing Becomes Her. The crux is in the first two bolts; once past, cruise to the anchors. 5 bolts.

FA: Eric Ebele, Tom Volo

14. Nothing's Left 5.8 ★★

Left line of the two on the face. A bouldery start leads to a lower angle face with big holds.

FA: Scott Aldinger, Lisa Schmitz

15. Nothing's Right 5.8 ★★

Right line of the two on the face. Getting off the ground is the crux of the route; after the second bolt it eases into jugs on a lower angle face.

FA: Scott Aldinger, Lisa Schmitz

16. Great Short Route 5.9 ★★

One of the first routes you'll encounter at the top of the short scramble up to The Holey Void. A fun, short route that starts off the ground on good holds next to a seam. The higher you get, the more beta intensive it becomes. 4 bolts.

FA: Fred AmRhein, Brandon Slemp

17. Chutes and Ladders 5.7 ★★

Start with jugs and stemming in the chimney. Pull onto the lower angle face and continue up the arete to the anchors. 7 bolts.

FA: Marty Karabin, Steve Shaffer

18. Mr. Boiler Man 5.10+ PG-13 (T)★

Climbs the crack to the left of Loc-Tite. Start in a thin crack in the dihedral and follow it up as it flares into a fist crack. Use the finger crack to gain the upper slab. Shares anchors with Loc-Tite. *Doubles .1-3, single 4, nuts.*

FA: Richie Winter

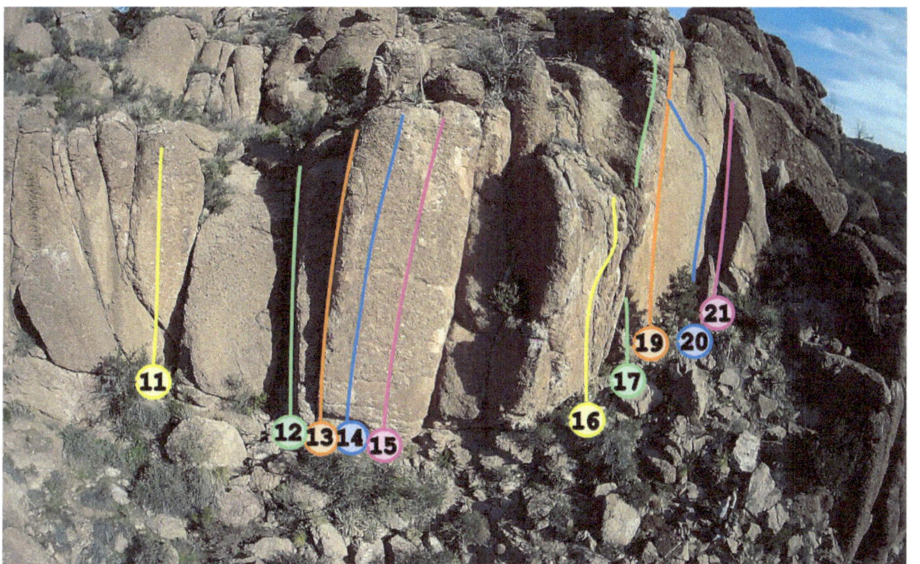

PHOTO: RICHARD REED

19. Loc-Tite 5.11c ★★★★

Left line on the smooth face by the small tree. Technical and sequential through the first four bolts -- utilize every thin foothold, mono, and small pocket available to you. After the intial crux pull over the bulge onto the slab and continue straight up to the anchors. 6 bolts.

FA: Marty Karabin, Bill Burns

20. Endomorph Man 5.12c/d ★★

Right line on the smooth face by the small tree. Similar to its neighbor to the left, only with smaller holds! Start up the thin, technical face to a very, very thought-provoking crux. After the fourth bolt, cut to the left. Shares the last bolt and anchors with Loc-Tite. 5 bolts, stick clip recommended.

FA: Craig Keaty

21. No Joshin' No Boschin' 5.6 (T)

Climbs the crack in the corner, next to the smooth face, up to a natural anchor. *SR.*

FA: Mike Kaczocha, Pat Metz, Greg Opland

UPPER POND WEST

☀ MORNING SHADE

From the rebar ladder, make your way across to the west side of the creek and follow the trail that traverses along the cliff. The furthest east routes in the west side of the Upper Pond can be found just after you scramble up a small boulder pile and just before the trail cuts behind a tree (a tree that is quite hard to miss as you have to step over the trunk). To get to the first routes listed (furthest west), continue on the trail until you come to the short scramble that winds up and around the corner to The Holey Void.

The west side of The Pond comes into the sun fairly early in the morning, and by mid-morning you can count on it being at least a few degrees warmer than anywhere else in the canyon by mid morning. In the winter, the walls will remain sunny until it's dark out but, in the shoulder seasons you'll have an hour or two of climbing in the shade before the sun dips below the horizon.

22. Fat Boy Goes To The Pond 5.6 ★★★

Climbs a short, heavily pocketed column. 3 bolts.

FA: Greg Opland, Felicia Terry

23. Dreaming of Chocolate Bunnies 5.8 ★★★

Furthest left line on the face next to Fat Boy Goes To The Pond. Climb the pocketed face past a bulge near the bottom and continue up the arete to the anchors. 6 bolts.

FA: Christopher Bastek, Michael Farrar, Stuart Speckner

24. Sappy Love Song 5.8 ★★

Follows the heavily pocketed face. Don't let the run out near the top get to your head! 4 bolts.

FA: Marty Karabin, Bills Burns

25. Follow Your Heart 5.8 ★★★

Right-most line on the face next to Fat Boy Goes To The Pond. Pocketed face to a tricky bulge near the top. 6 bolts.

FA: Fred AmRhein, Donna Forest, Gene Reeck

26. Christmas Chocolate 5.7 ★★

Starts immediately to the right of Follow Your Heart. Climb up and over a big bulge to a rewarding lower angle face. 6 bolts.

FA: Fred AmRhein, Donna Forest, Gene Reeck

27. God Save the Ta Tas 5.8 ★

A somewhat difficult, bouldery start leads to a pocketed face with good rests. 7 bolts.

FA: Fred AmRhein

28. The Overlooked Chimney 5.7 (T)

Infrequently climbed, so don't be too dismayed to find it has collected its fair share of dirt, rocks, and branches. Classic chimneying will get you up to the tree, then transition into a wide stem to anchors shared with Casting Couch. *Doubles .5-2, nuts.*

FA: Unknown

29. The Casting Couch 5.9 ★★★

Climbs the face, using the arete, just to the right of the wide chimney. Near the seventh bolt traverse a little further right to stick to the face. 9 bolts.

FA: Ronnie Miller, Christopher Bastek, Thomas Park

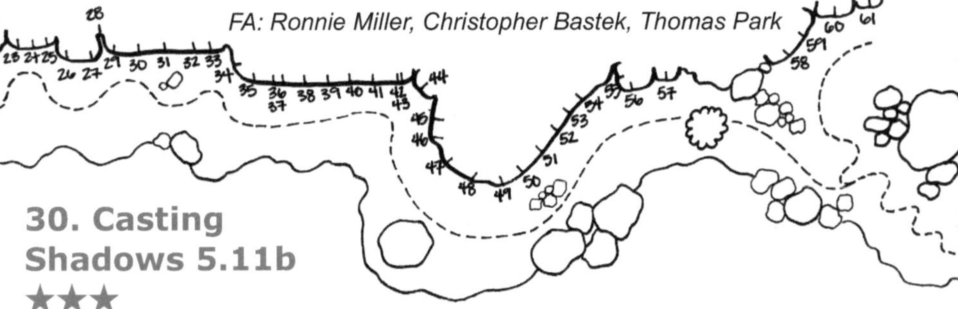

30. Casting Shadows 5.11b ★★★

Thin, technical and relentless! Climbs the face just to the right of Casting Couch. A tough as nails crux down low leads to more small pockets and crimps right till the very end. 7 bolts.

FA: Craig Keaty, Michelle Lepinsky

31. In Seam 5.10c ★★★

Just to the right of Casting Shadows, In Seam follows the obvious vertical seam with a cruxy bit just before the horizontal break. 8 bolts.

FA: Fred AmRhein

32. Nothing Lasts Forever 5.10d ★★

Start on a bulge and pull through a lower cruxy bit. Take advantage of the rests you can find down low and save a bit for the higher crux by the horizontal seam. 9 bolts.

FA: Lisa Barnes, Scott Aldinger

33. Close Call 5.10c ★★

Climbs the bolt line to the left of the corner crack system. Follows pockets and crimps up the broken face. 9 bolts.

FA: Fred AmRhein, Gene Reeck

34. The Big Weld Show 5.11a ★★★★

A route that has a little bit of everything! To the right of the corner crack system. Climb up to the ledge before pulling through the overhang on a healthy combination of jugs and crimps. Enjoy a rest before heading up the thin face on great edges and pockets. 11 bolts.

FA: Fred AmRhein, Gene Reeck

35. Adamantasaurus Flacciphallicus PhD 5.11b ★★

Just around the corner from The Big Weld Show. A bouldery start gains you access to a technical face with quite a few bulges. 11 bolts.

FA: Fred AmRhein Christopher Bastek

36. Bubbalisa 5.11b ★

Climbs the thin crack just to the right of Mona Lisa. Toward the top, step onto the bolted line and finish on Mona Lisa. .3-2, nuts.

FA: Chris Raypole, Sandy Draus

37. Mona Lisa 5.11b ★★★★

The bolted chute on the far left side of the wall. Stem up the dihedral to the overhanging, cruxy crack. Utilize every trick in your book -- fingerlocking, lie backing, jamming -- to get over the bulge at the top. 9 bolts.

FA: Fred AmRhein, Michelle AmRhein, Leo Bunuel, Chris Raypole

PHOTO: RICHARD REED

38. Time Share 5.12a/b ★★

Start on the thin face to the right of Mona Lisa. The higher you get the crispier the holds become. Delicate face climbing; if the typical pocket-pulling of the area is wearing on you, you might enjoy the chance of pace. 10 bolts.

FA: Fred AmRhein, Gene Reeck

39. Blisters In The Sun 5.12a ★★★★

Fun, delicate face climbing. Thin edges and small pockets lead to the middle of the route, where some thoughtful edging will get you on your way. 10 bolts.

FA: Fred AmRhein, Sandy Draus, David Dodemaide

40. Bartuni 5.11c/d PG-13

An easily identified route, due to the outrageous mess of glue around each bolt coupled with zero chalk on any of the holds. Start on a less than vertical face and trend up and right toward the cruxy bulges near the anchors -- do your very best to not fall here. 10 bolts.

FA: Chris Werner

41. The Soft Parade 5.11b ★★★★

An area classic! Start on a less than vertical face then head up the seam on crimps and small pockets until you gain a ledge. From there trend left to pull over the first bulge and back right to pull the second. Fun movement on great rock. 10 bolts.

FA: Marty Karabin

42. The Ball 5.10d ★★★

Just to the right of The Soft Parade. Head up the less than vertical face and clip the first bolt from the ball in the seam. Continue up the face and arete on great pockets and a few crimps to anchors on the ledge. Stay off the wall to the right unless you want to cheat yourself out of the fun. 7 bolts.

FA: Cas Sundell, Charlie Brown

43. And Chain 5.11c/d ★★★

An extension to The Ball. If you wanna go for the full ball and chain, clip the anchor for The Ball (the minor drag this creates is well worth it to keep the rope in) and continue up the thin, technical face. 3 bolts.

FA: Cas Sundell, Charlie Brown

44. Adventure Quest 5.8 ★★

True to its name. Adventure up ledges and pocketed faces in the corner to the left of Pocket Puzzle. A few thoughtful moves on jugs at the top moving out of the chimney and back onto the face. 8 bolts.

FA: Marty Karabin

45. Pocket Puzzle 5.10a ★★★★

A fantastic, steep face with an overabundance of pockets that can truly make it feel like a puzzle. The crux is in the first two bolts; once past it's just a matter of finding the pockets you want to use and jetting up. Located on the west-facing wall just around the corner from the big roof, the route stays shady quite a bit longer than its neighbors. 8 bolts.

FA: Craig Keaty

46. Arete Horizon 5.10a ★★★★

Reminiscent of its neighbor to the left. Climbs the face just to the right of Pocket Puzzle, occasionally utilizing the arete. 9 bolts.

FA: Chris Bastek, Eric Agaciewski

47. Any Horizon 5.11c ★★★★

One of the very few steep 11s at The Pond. Clip the first bolt of Arete Horizon before traversing out right on a large rail. Pull over the roof and continue up the overhanging face on nice pockets and crimps. Shares anchors with Just Can't Get Any. 4 bolts.

FA: Charlie Brown

48. Just Can't Get Any 5.12c/d ★★★

A fairly short line that climbs the intimidating overhang to the right of Pocket Puzzle. Start off a pinch and move onto the rail before heading up the steep face, mostly on crimps. 4 bolts.

FA: Greg Varella, Chad Cooper

49. Rocky Horror Picture Show 5.10d ★★

To the right of the big overhang. Trends up and left through a series of small overhangs and bulges. 10 bolts.

FA: Marty Karabin, William Haeberle, Bill Paul

50. Pocket Pulling Pansies 5.10a ★★

Start near the right-leaning crack and head up the steep, pocketed face. 7 bolts.

FA: Eric Agaciewski, Chris Bastek, Steve Dison

51. Pocket Party 5.10b ★★

Starts to the right of the right-leaning crack off a large boulder. As the name implies, more pocket-pulling fun. 7 bolts.

FA: Brad Mattingly, Mark Trainor

52. Space Hog 5.10c ★★

The middle line on the south facing wall. A bit crimpy down low but you'll be rewarded with bigger holds as you go. It is a bit of a double-edged sword however, as the higher you go the steeper it gets. 8 bolts.

FA: Fred AmRhein

53. Pocket Pow Wow 5.10b ★★

Head up on crimpy pockets and follow the good ones, trending slightly left and then back right, before reaching the anchors. 5 bolts.

FA: Fred AmRhein, Michelle AmRhein, Greg Opland, Leo Bunuei, Scott Aldinger, Felica Terry

54. Main Squeeze 5.11a ★★

Furthest right route on the south facing wall. A short, albeit quite pumpy, pocketed face. 6 bolts.

FA: Craig Keaty

55. Pocket Warmer 5.6 ★★

A west-facing, off-vertical face with big pockets on a separate pillar to the right of Main Squeeze. 5 bolts.

FA: Fred AmRhein

56. Pockets Are Stronger Than Partners 5.7 ★

Start on the same pedestal as for Pocket Warmer, but step right onto the big foothold and head up and right toward your first bolt. From there head straight up on positive holds and over a final bulge.

FA: Ronnie Miller

57. Gatekeeper 5.10 a/b ★

Around the corner from Pocket Warmer on a separate pillar. Start with virtually no feet and high hands. The trickiest moves are in the beginning; once you get your feet on the wall and pull over the bulge you'll be into easier climbing. 5 bolts.

FA: Ross Cowan, Brett Digwood

58. Cowboy 5.10a ★★

From the main trail scramble up a few boulders on a less than obvious trail to gain access to the slightly overhanging wall. Cowboy is the furthest left route on the wall. Head up a slab with positive holds to a high first bolt then up the steep face. 3 bolts.

FA: Chad Cooper

59. Cowgirl 5.9 ★★★★

Just to the left of Cowboy. Start up the vertical face -- get ready to turn it on as the angle increases about halfway up. Fun movement on big pockets and sidepulls. 4 bolts.

FA: Marty Karabin, Robert Olson, Bill Paul

60. Leave Your Money On The Dresser 5.10b ★★

Lone route to the right of the corner, slightly uphill from Cowboy and Cowgirl. A fun, tricky overhanging route. 3 bolts.

FA: Bill Paul, Marty Karabin, Robert Olson

61. Pony Express 5.5 ★

A low angle, short, fun route just around the corner from Leave Your Money On The Dresser.

FA: Robert Olson, Bill Paul, Marty Karabin

UPPER POND EAST

☀ MORNING SHADE

The Upper Pond East is hosts some of the hardest routes in the area as well as a good handful of moderates. Most of the routes are situated right next to the pond, making them a few degrees cooler (and a few decibels louder) when the waterfall is flowing. To get to the furthest left routes in the area make your way to the west side of the creek and head uphill via the web of trails just a short way.

Routes #62 - #80 are on the west side of the pond,
routes #81 - #92 are to the east.

The east side of The Pond comes into the sun almost first thing in the morning but by mid to late afternoon returns to the shade.

62. Kitty Litter 5.9 ★★

Left bolt line of the two on the well pocketed face. Start up the juggy flake to the sloping ledge and then jet up the last few bolts as the angle of the wall gradually increases. 4 bolts.

FA: Paul Dief, KC

63. The Warden 5.10b ★★

Just to the right of Kitty Litter and the obvious flake. Start up thin face climbing to the first bolt then continue up the pocketed, vertical face. Stay off the wall behind you! 4 bolts.

FA: Craig Keaty

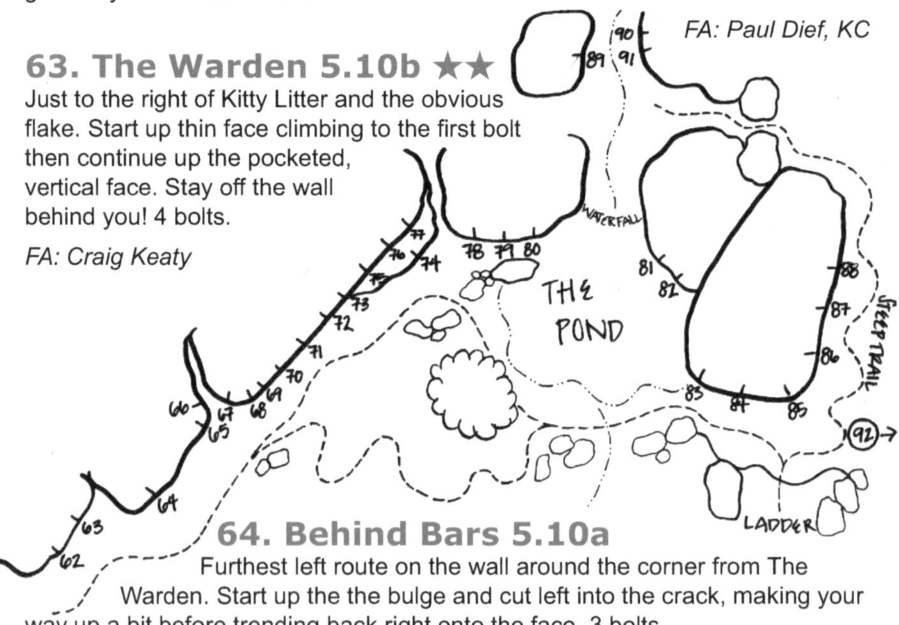

64. Behind Bars 5.10a

Furthest left route on the wall around the corner from The Warden. Start up the the bulge and cut left into the crack, making your way up a bit before trending back right onto the face. 3 bolts.

FA: Craig Keaty

65. Wild Wild West 5.11b ★★

Short line just outside of the wide chimney. Start up the ramp to gain access to the small overhang then pull up into the fun crux sequence. 4 bolts.

FA: Marty Karabin

66. Winds of Change 5.8 ★
Low angle face with big holds just around the corner from Wild Wild West. 4 bolts.

FA: Marty Karabin

67. Weak Sister 5.10a ★★
Climbs the face to the right of the wide chimney. A tough start up the face, but keep off the wall behind you. After the second bolt traverse out right over a crack then continue up the face to the anchors. 6 bolts.

FA: Ken Mills, Dave Sobocan

68. Out on Parole 5.10c ★★
Start up the slab and onto an overhanging, rounded arete. 5 bolts.

FA: Craig Keaty

69. Pompasfuc 5.12b ★
Start the same as for Out on Parole. Cut right after the third bolt and head up through the two bolt crux. Shares anchors with Out on Parole. 5 bolts.

FA: Aaron Draude, Aaron Adams

70. Open Project
Seven bolt overhanging face to the left of The Emerald established by Craig Keaty in 1994.

71. The Emerald 5.13d ★★
The line just left of center. Climbs the overhanging face on small pockets and even smaller crimps. 7 bolts.

FA: Craig Keaty

72. Desert Devil 5.13b ★★★★
Climbs the center of the sweeping overhang. A consummate enduro-fest with a V4 immediately off the deck and a heartbreaker V3 right at the very end. 8 bolts.

FA: Craig Keaty

73. Death Row 5.12d ★★

Just to the left of the crack and water streak on the overhanging face. Fun moves to good pockets, but the angle will inevitably build on ya! 7 bolts.

FA: Craig Keaty EB: Jim Steagall, Diedre Burton

74. Gatekeeper 5.9 ★

This route was intended as a way to access routes #75-#77 on the overhang above but is equipped to be climbed on its own as well. Below the water-stained overhang climb the vertical face to slab. 5 bolts.

FA: Craig Keaty

75. Hot Line 5.12d ★★

To the right of the water-stained crack. Head up the furthest left line of the three that depart from the Gatekeeper anchors on the ledge. An overhanging, crimpy line that can be quite slippery after a good rain. 5 bolts.

FA: Craig Keaty

76. Hot House 5.12c ★

The center line that departs from the ledge. 6 bolts.

FA: Craig Keaty EB: Ken Mills

77. Mistaken Identity 5.12a ★★

Furthest right line that departs from the ledge with the anchors for Gatekeeper. Keep off the wall behind you. 6 bolts.

FA: Craig Keaty EB: Greg Varella

78. Young and Reckless 5.7 R ★

Leftmost line on the vertical face directly left of the pond. Shares the first bolt with Easy Pool. A few thinner moves in the beginning lead to a vertical jug-haul the rest of the way but beware -- the size of the holds won't mitigate the back to back fifteen foot runouts, and a fall almost anywhere would deposit you on the ground or a ledge. 6 bolts.

FA: Jeff Giek, Gordon Ogden

79. Easy Pool 5.7 ★★

Middle line on the vertical face directly left of the pond. Shares the first bolt with Young and Reckless. Pull onto the ledge and head up the face. Thinner opening moves lead to large, incut pockets and edges the rest of the way. 9 bolts.

FA: Unknown

80. Dead Pool 5.8 ★★

Rightmost route on the vertical face directly left of the pond. Start on the boulder at the edge of the pond and step across the gap onto the face above the water. Two bolts lead to a ledge then continuous climbing on thin but positive holds bring you to the anchors. A fun, aesthetic line. 10 bolts. *Originally established as a 5.8 X mixed line by Leo Bunuel and Steve Shultz in 1990 and later reconfigured in 2007 into the much more enjoyable sport line that it is today.*

FA: Marty Karabin

To get to routes #81 - #91: From the rebar ladder keep to the east side of the creek and head straight up the very steep trail, if it can be called that. Depending on which route you're looking to climb cut left down low to gain access to the big ledge underneath the roof or continue scrambling up to the top of the pillar.

81. Drowning 5.10a ★

Climbs the slick face directly above the east side of the pond. Start by rapping in to a hanging belay and climb out the water polished face. 5 bolts.

FA: Ken Mills, Matt Krise

82. Big Legged Woman 5.10b ★

Climbs the slick face directly above the east side of the pond. Rap in to gain access to a hanging belay and climb out the water polished face. 5 bolts.

FA: Ken Mills, Matt Krise

83. Inner Basin 5.10c ★★

Traverse out the big ledge underneath the large overhang to a single bolt belay anchor on the far left side. Climbs the furthest left line that can be accessed from the ledge. Follow the bolt line over the water, trending right, to the top of the pillar. There's no anchors designated for this line. Belay your second up via the anchors for Natural Wonder, walk off. 5 bolts.

FA: Bill Paul

84. Interloper 5.11b/c ★

From the single bolt belay on the big ledge underneath the large overhang, stick clip the first bolt and head up and left, just barely circumventing the roof on steep ground, before moving straight up to the anchors. The start might be a bit crunchy but the rock quality improves the higher you get. 8 bolts.

FA: Greg Mayer

85. Natural Wonder 5.8 (T) ★

Follows the large crack to the right of the big roof. Start in a good hand crack and continue up as the crack widens to a two bolt anchor. *Doubles 3-6 (or as many big cams as you can scrounge together).*

FA: Marty Karabin, Bill Burns

86. Crazy Fingers 5.11c ★★

First bolted line on the east-facing wall to the right of the big roof. Thin, smooth vertical face. If you climb past the first set of anchors you encounter, you'll be met with the anchors for Natural Wonder which you'll find are quite a bit newer. 5 bolts, stick clip recommended.

FA: Gordon Ogden, Russ Keith

87. El Gato Grande D'Amore 5.12a ★★

Middle bolted line on the east-facing wall, to the right of the big roof. Thin, seemingly impossible face with holds just where you need them. Head up the smooth face to the large overhang right before the last bolt. 4 bolts, stick clip recommended.

FA: Chad Cooper

88. Beer and Dead Animals 5.9 ★

Furthest right line on the east-facing wall, to the right of the big roof. Heavily pocketed, short route. 2 bolts.

FA: Bill Paul

89. The Toad Warrior 5.12b ★

At the top of the waterfall on the west side of the creek. Steep, thin face to the first bolt. Pull over a bulge onto the vertical, more featured face and continue up the left-leaning line to the anchors. 3 bolts.

FA: Chad Cooper

90. Primordial Soup 5.11a ★★

At the very top of the waterfall on the east side of the creek. Overhanging, thin crack to the left of Coronary Bypass. When the route was established there was a tree for the belay -- a tree that, sadly, seems to no longer exist. Bring some extra gear for the anchor and plan to scramble off the top. .3-2.

FA: Chris Raypole, Chris Pomeroy

91. Coronary Bypass 5.10b ★★

At the top of the waterfall on the east side of the creek. A bold first bolt leads to an overhanging scoop to a bulge and eventually an off-vertical face. 4 bolts.

FA: Jeff Giek, Gordon Ogden

92. Queen Anne 5.11a ★

From the top of the rebar ladder, cut right and follow a faint trail for a hundred feet around the corner to this lone route. Sustained, pocketed face. 9 bolts.

FA: Jesper Osher

LOWER POND

☀ EVENING SHADE

From the parking area hike east to the Waterfall Bridge and cross underneath the highway. All the routes are a short way uphill on the west side of the creek. The Lower Pond comes into the sun almost first thing in the morning, but by the mid to late afternoon it will come back into the shade.

93. The Crosses Are Free 5.10c ★★

Furthest left bolt line at the Lower Pond. Start on the face between the two vertical seams, trending slightly left for the first few bolts, then straight up the vertical face. 7 bolts.

FA: Fred AmRhein

94. Youth Is Beauty 5.10b ★★

Start to the right of the vertical seam. Climb the rounded arete and crimpy face. 11 bolts.

FA: Fred AmRhein

95. Ponyo 5.8+ PG-13 (T)

Just to the left of Return From the Great Mormon Experience. Varied climbing follows the discontinuous crack system past several ledges. While there's many holds on the face, most of them should have been cleaned, so it's in your best interest to avoid trusting them. It's in your belayer's best interest to wear a helmet. Shares anchors with Return From the Great Mormon Experience. *Doubles .3-4.*

FA: Jacob Mamiya

96. Return From the Great Mormon Experience 5.12b ★★★★

Start by scrambling up onto a boulder and then stem over to the first bolt. From there avoid stemming back and keep on the thin face as a few difficult, technical sections bring you to the crux. Once you're past the deadpoint, shake out and finish up the second half of the route on jugs. 10 bolts.

FA: Chad Cooper

97. Rock Lobster 5.10a ★

Start downhill and just around the corner from Return From the Great Mormon Experience. Fun, interesting moves through an open book and a crux down low lead to a vertical face at the top, with some thoughtful moves around the last bolt. 8 bolts.

FA: Marty Karabin

98. Clueless 5.11c ★

Start just downhill from Rock Lobster. Gain a ledge down low then follow the scoop to another ledge and up a vertical face to the anchors. 9 bolts.

FA: Marty Karabin

99. Ninja School 5.10d ★

Start by the obvious right leaning seam. Follow four bolts to a ledge then head up a more continuous, bulgy face. 9 bolts.

FA: Marty Karabin

100. Liquid Sunshine 5.10c ★

Stem past a bolt to gain a ledge then jet up the bulgy face to the anchors. 5 bolts.

FA: Greg Opland, Russ Keith

101. Noah's Ark 5.10c ★

From the top of the boulder head up a vertical face, passing over a wide crack into a fun corner system. 7 bolts.

FA: Marty Karabin

102. Takin' It To The Street 5.9 ★★★

Thoughtful climbing on the broken face over several bulges. Finishes on a more delicate slab. 9 bolts.

FA: Marty Karabin

THE HARBOR

Directly across the canyon from the upper area of The Pond sits The Harbor, a newer addition to the canyon. A small crag with more of the classic pocket pulling that Queen Creek Canyon is known for as well as, more notably, an unusually smooth, extremely dense face with perfect cracks and bulletproof crimps.
Most of the routes at The Harbor stay in the shade all day.

GETTING THERE

From Superior, take US-60 east for 3 miles. Park at the third pull off on the south side of the highway, the same parking as for The Pond.

From Globe, take US-60 west for 21 miles and park at the pull off on the south side of the road, just after the small bridge.
(33.30846, 111.07089)

From the upper east side of the pull off drop down into the creek and head up the hill on the other side, following a distinct trail up to the base of the crag.

THE SHIP

☀ MORNING SHADE

The Ship is the west-facing, pocketed wall that sits above the largish, flat area you encounter at the end of the trail. While it's definitely not the best rock in the canyon, the routes are a good warm up for the lines at The Dock.

Walk a short ways up from the flat pad on a less than obvious trail. The trail cuts left a little early before circling back right to the base of the routes.

1. The Bow 5.11a ★

Furthest left line on the wall. Start directly below the arete. Climb up and over several lips to a no hands rest just before the distinct boulder problem. 6 bolts.

FA: Steven Neveadomi

2. Ocean Man 5.10d ★

Just to the right of the arete. Sustained, delicate moves on thin crimps and sharp pockets. 4 bolts.

FA: Steven Neveadomi

PHOTO: STEVEN NEVEADOMI

3. Portside 5.10a ★

Climbs directly up the middle of the wall. Great movement on a variety of holds. 5 bolts.

FA: Steven Neveadomi, Marty Moore

4. The Minnow 5.6

A short line that climbs the distinctly blocky, fractured face. 3 bolts.

FA: Paul Paonessa, Vincent Batista

5. The Mast 5.9

The tallest line on the wall. Start on sidepulls before traversing onto a blockier face, where thought-provoking moves on better rock bring you to the anchor. 5 bolts.

FA: Steven Neveadomi

THE DOCK

ALL DAY SHADE

The Dock is the unmistakable, smooth face at the end of the trail. Stellar routes on stellar rock combined with the permenant shade make it one of the best places to spend a warmer day in Queen Creek.

6. Stuffed Sea Cucumber 5.11b ★★

Climbs the left arete. Start on the far left end of the main face and head straight up into the crux. Shares anchors with The Cracken. 6 bolts.

FA: Nate Poleway
EB: Steven Neveadomi

PHOTO: STEVEN NEVEADOMI

7. The Cracken 5.11c ★★★★

Climbs the fantastic crack up the center of the wall. Amazing movement -- this climb alone would make the hike up to the crag well worth it. Utilize the crack in every way you can think of. 6 bolts.

FA: Sarah Teater
EB: Steven Neveadomi

8. Keelhaul 5.12b ★★★

A stunning line on sloping rails, thin sidepulls and even thinner seams. Hard as nails, be sure to warm your fingers up beforehand. 6 bolts.

FA: Charlie Brown

9. Castaway 5.11c ★★★

Rightmost line on the formation. Super thin moves to steep jugs. 5 bolts.

FA: Cas Sundell, Charlie Brown

DIAMOND BUTTRESS

Diamond Buttress is a small collection of routes on a short cliff close (but not too close!) to the highway. The rock is solid and the bolts, when there are bolts, are bomber.

The whole area sees sun for a few hours when the sun comes up then stays shaded from the late morning until the end of the day.

GETTING THERE

From Superior, take US-60 east for 3.5 miles and park on the fourth pull out on the south side of the road.

From Globe, take US-60 west for 20.5 miles and park on the pull out on the south side of the road, half a mile before the small bridge.
(33.30935, 111.06249)

From there follow a fairly obvious trail down into the wash and follow the cairns up the slab to the short wall that can be seen from the road.

1. Grim Ripper 5.11b/c ★★

Climbs the east-facing side of the buttress with a diamond-shaped face. Follow small pockets up the slightly overhanging face. Originally a project abandoned in 1989, it was later sent in 1996. 4 bolts.

FA: Kevin Benson, Issac Hingley

2. Ja Ja Ding Dong 5.7 (T) ★

Just around the corner from Grim Ripper. Follow a discontinuous crack. Start in the wide crack at the bottom to a bolted face in the middle and finish up a crack that angles left and cuts underneath the roof. *3 bolts, SR.*

FA: Aaron Collins

3. Greeley 5.8 (T) ★★

Wide, obvious zigzagging crack. *SR, 4.*

FA: Kent Brock, Don O'Kelley

4. Monster Trucks 5.12a ★★

Scramble up an easy slab to a high first bolt next to a broken crack. Climbs the overhanging arete. Avoid stemming in the dihedral down low after the first bolt is clipped; stick to the sloping arete. 6 bolts.

FA: Austin Hancock

5. Elf Attack 5.4

Climbs the obvious slab-angled face in the right-facing dihedral. 3 bolts.

FA: Aaron Collins

Routes #6 -#8 are located in a narrow corridor a few hundred feet north of the buttress with a diamond-shaped face. Once upon a time, the large boulder that makes up the north side of the corridor had a large Budweiser emblem painted onto it, before the state came through and sandblasted the graffiti off the walls. Even though it's been gone since the 90's, the name Budweiser Boulder has stuck around.

6. Unknown Route

Climbs the thin arete to the left of Artemis past 3 bolts.

7. Artemis 5.12b PG-13 ★★

Bolt line in the middle of the narrow corridor. Starts on a rail then heads up into small pockets that only decrease in size and depth the higher you get. 4 bolts.

FA: Richie Winter

8. Most Excellent B.S. 5.10d R

Furthest right bolt line in the narrow corridor. A thin face to a mantle at the top. Falling just before or on the mantle would be a very bad idea. Shares anchors with Artemis. 2 bolts.

FA: Marc Nielsen, Lanny Johns

Routes #9 - #12 are located just around the corner from the Budweiser boulder. A steep slab runs from the creek to a small ledge at the base of the wall.

9. Volcano Man 5.10a ★

Thin arete. While the rock is heavily featured in some stretches, the good holds can be a little harder to find. 4 bolts.

FA: Aaron Collins

10. Sucker Pockets From Hell 5.10b ★★

A stiff, bolted face that got it's name for a reason. Runout to the anchors, although there is a thin crack that would easily take gear. 3 bolts.

FA: Jeff Giek, Matt Hudson, Leo Bunuel

11. Danish Girls Make Pastries 5.10c ★★

Starts in a short dihedral. Continue up the bolted face to a crack at the top. A small piece of gear alleviates the runout to the anchors. 2 bolts.

FA: Jeff Giek, Matt Hudson, Leo Bunuel

12. Midnight Express 5.11b ★

A challenging but fun, short face to a bulge at the top. 4 bolts.

FA: Ken Mills

13. Tips 5.11a ★★

Furthest right bolt line (next to the boulder with the glued eyelets). Thin, positive edges and small pockets up a vertical face. 4 bolts.

FA: Richie Winter, Aaron Collins, Soren Stauersbol

14. Tricam Monster 5.6 (T)

Crack next to the tree to the right of Tips. Climb past ledges and a single bolt to anchors. *.3-2 (and tricams if you prefer).*

FA: Aaron Collins, Soren Stauersbol

Routes #15 - #17 are located on a wall around the corner and to the left of the rest of Diamond Buttress. You can cut across ledges and lower down onto the belay ramp for these routes, but most would argue that it's easier to just hike down into the wash, walk downstream a few yards, and hike back up.

15. Criss Cross Applesauce 5.9 ★

Follows the right leaning crack.

FA: Trevor H, Aaron Collins, Bob C

16. Life Twists 5.10a ★

Follows the thin seam in the center of the wall.

FA: Aaron Collins, Soren Stauersbol

17. Betty Davis Eyes 5.9 ★

Furthest left bolt line, just left of the crack system.

FA: Aaron Collins, Betty Nunez

WOUNDED KNEE WALL

The Wounded Knee Wall is a collection of short routes, most of which are easier, old school cracks put up in the late 70's and early 80's. As most of the cracks have gear belays and walk offs it's easy to set up top ropes on these routes, making it a great area to practice your crack climbing or gear placements.

GETTING THERE

From Superior, take US-60 east for 3.5 miles and park on the fourth pull out on the south side of the road.

From Globe, take US-60 west for 20.5 miles and park on the pull out on the south side of the road, half a mile before the small bridge.
(33.30935, 111.06249)

Same as the pull off for Diamond Buttress.

From the pull off look to the southeast side of the creek.

SOUTH SIDE WALL

☀ MORNING SHADE

From the pull out look for the furthest east outcropping of stone along the southeast side of the wash. The approach might be a bit of a bushwhack, but at least it's short-lived.

1. Light Duty 5.6 (T)

Climbs the broken crack system at the very left end of the wall. Walk off. SR..

FA: Don O'Kelley, Kent Brock

2. Straight Up 5.8 (T)

A few hundred feet to the right of Light Duty. Starts off a large block and climbs the thin, vertical crack, passing through quite a few horizontals. Walk off. *SR.*

FA: Don O'Kelley, Kent Brock

3. Two Hands 5.7 (T)

Starts off the opposite end of the large block from Straight Up. Climb up the face to gain access to two left-leaning thin cracks. Follow the cracks as they trend slightly right before cutting back left to the top. Walk off. *SR.*

FA: Don O'Kelley, Kent Brock

4. Ray Ray 5.7 (T)

Climbs the crack in the dihedral just to the right of Two Hands. Walk off. *SR.*

FA: Kent Brock, Don O'Kelley

5. Ray Way 5.7 (T)

To the right of the shallow dihedral, follow the crack that trends slightly to the right before heading straight up to the top. Walk off. *SR.*

FA: Kent Brock, Don O'Kelley

TERRY + TERRY WALL

☀ MORNING SHADE

Located southeast from the pull off across the creek.

6. Terry + Terry 5.10a

Bolted face to the right of a pillar. Walk off. 3 bolts.

FA: Unknown

7. Deception 5.7 (T)

Climbs the crack to the right of the 3 bolt face. Trends to the left near the top. Walk off. *SR.*

FA: Kent Brock, Don O'Kelley

WOUNDED KNEE WALL

☀ MORNING SHADE

From the pull out, drop down into the wash and follow it south for a few hundred feet. The wall will be on your left.

8. Abandoned Dreams 5.12c ★

On the very left end of the wall and slightly around the corner you'll find this north facing short route. Follows a thin face to a bulge at the top. 2 bolts.

FA: Jay Anderson Jr

9. Wounded Pride 5.10a PG-13 (T) ★

Start the same as for Wounded Knee, but when you reach the ramp cut left to head out past the roof. *.2-2.*

FA: Scott Duemler, Amber Abomb

10. Wounded Knee 5.10a (T) ★

Starts behind a large tree. Follow the overhanging crack in the dihedral to a ramp near the top. Walk off. *.2-3.*

FA: Kent Brock, Don O'Kelley, Jay Watts

11.Crazy Horse 5.7 (T) ★

Climbs the chimney into the double cracks. Walk off or rap Abandoned Dreams. *.2-3.*

FA: Kent Brock, Don O'Kelley

12. Standing Bull 5.9 (T) ★

Follows a thin crack on the face to the right of the chimney. Walk off or rap Abandoned Dreams. *.2-1, nuts.*

FA: Kent Brock, Don O"Kelley

13. Bwana Vists Queen Creek 5.9

Thin, pocketed face. 4 bolts.

FA; Jeffrey "Bwana" Jones, Jim Boca, Seese

14. Gray's First 5.6 (T)

Just to the right of the short bolted face. Follow the crack in the left facing dihedral to the top. Walk off or rap Abandoned Dreams. *.3-2.*

FA: Kent Brock, Don O'Kelley

15. Bury My Corazon 5.8 (T)

Climbs the rounded arete just to the right of Gray's First. Don't expect much good pro. Walk off.

FA: Todd Swain

16. Heaven Sent Brent 5.7 (T) ★

Starts to the right of the rounded arete. Climb past one bolt and into a left leaning crack. *.3-2.*

FA: Jeffrey "Bwana" Jones, Jim Boca, Seese

17. Heaven Sent Brent Variation 5.10c (T)

After the bolt cut right into a crack and follow it to the top. *.3-2.*

FA: Jeffrey "Bwana" Jones, Jim Boca, Seese

RESOURCES

THE FIGHT FOR OAK FLAT

To learn more about the fight for Oak Flat, how you can help, and for more recent updates, you can visit the websites curated by the Apache Stronghold, the Access Fund, and the AMRC.

apache-stronghold.com
accessfund.org/action-alerts/save-oak-flat
azminingreform.org/t/oak-flat

REBOLTING

In your time in the canyon you may notice the varying age of bolts, ranging anywhere from brand new to 30+ years old. In the past handful of years, there has been an effort to replace any and all of the aging bolts but this, of course, takes time and money. If interested in donating or getting involved, feel free to reach out to casandthesun@gmail.com.

PHOTOS

FRONT COVER
Alice Held on Deadpool, photo by Jackson Sims-Myers
Jaci Teresinski on Desert Devil, photo by Sydney Tunell
Richie Winter on KingFisher, photo by Jacob Mamiya

BACK COVER
Scott McDaniel on Nothing's Left, photo by Zach Duncan

TABLE OF CONTENTS
Scott McDaniel on Nothing's Left, photo by Zach Duncan
Javier Garcia on Desert Devil, photo by Jacob Mamiya

THE OLD HIGHWAY (P. 6 - 7)
Photo by Zach Duncan
John Mudd on Rage Bait, photo by Charlie Brown
Photo by Zach Duncan
Matthew Dion on Mansplaining, photo by Charlie Brown
Photo by Zach Duncan

ATLANTIS (P. 12 - 13)
Daniel Conrad on Corral of Voices, photo by Matt Heinen
Aaron Peterson on Rocket Man, photo by Unknown
Photo by Cas Sundell
Jim Steagall on the first ascent of Smokin' Guns, photo by Dave Sobocan
Scott McDaniel on G-String, photo by Zach Duncan

LITTLE ENGLAND WALL (P. 34)
Frank Vers on Zeus, photo by Sosa

QUEEN SCEPTER (P. 40)
Photo by Sam Boyle
Craig Keaty on Gripping the Universe, photo by Unknown

THE POND (P. 42 - 43)
Scott McDaniel on Deadpool, photo by Zach Duncan
Craig Keaty on The Emerald, photo by Unknown
Craig Keaty on Scorpion [Sunday School Wall, Off Limits], photo by Unknown
Jaci Teresinski on Desert Devil, photo by Sydney Tunell
Author on Loc Tite, photo by Matt Johnson

THE HARBOR (P. 61)
Photo by Steven Neveadomi
Charlie Brown on The Cracken

DIAMOND BUTTRESS (P. 64)
Aaron Peterson on Sir Charles, photo by Pieter Anthony Youngman

Noah Geiger on Unknown Route, photo by Jacob Bush

WOUNDED KNEE WALL (P. 68)

Micha Good on Nothing's Left
Tristen Martinex on Severed Member, photo by Jacob Bush

P. 72

Photo by Zach Duncan

www.ingramcontent.com/pod-product-compliance
Lightning Source LLC
LaVergne TN
LVHW052308100826
845147LV00006B/704